WRITING FOR YOUNG ADULTS

WRITING FOR YOUNG ADULTS

SHERRY GARLAND

WRITER'S DIGEST BOOKS
CINCINNATI, OHIO

Other fine Writer's Digest books are available from your local bookstore or direct from the publisher.

For information on more resources for writers, visit our Web site at www.write rsdigest.com.

To receive a free biweekly E-mail newsletter delivering tips and updates about writing and about Writer's Digest products, send an E-mail with "Subscribe Newsletter" in the body of the message to newsletter-request@writers digest.com, or register directly at our Web site at www.writersdigest.com.

02 01 00 99 98   5 4 3 2 1

Library of Congress Cataloging-in-Publication Data

Garland, Sherry.
    Writing for young adults / Sherry Garland.—1st ed.
      p.   cm.
    Includes bibliographical references (p.   ) and index.
    ISBN 0-89879-857-4 (pbk. : alk. paper)
    1. Young adult literature—Authorship. I. Title.
PN147.5.G37   1998
808.06'8—dc21   98-37787
                                        CIP

Edited by David Borcherding
Production edited by Amy J. Wolgemuth
Cover designed by Stephanie Redman
Cover illustrated by Anni Matsick

TABLE OF CONTENTS

As I was organizing the stacks of note cards that had accumulated while conducting research for this book, I found a card that simply stated: *There are no rules.* I must have jotted that down the day I realized that every rule I had read in how-to books was a rule I had broken. But after talking to people in writers groups and to fellow authors, I realized that although there may be no rules, at least there are some guidelines most writers agree with. These guidelines come after years of writing, selling and surviving in the publishing industry.

Not everyone reading this book will be on the same level of development. Basically, there are eleven stages writers go through before becoming successful authors. See if one of these fits you.

Stage One—Dreaming. You read voraciously, love words and language, and admire authors. You have great ideas that might make good young adult books but, for one reason or another, you haven't written anything down. You are "thinking about writing a book."

Stage Two—Planning. You finally get some words down on paper and tinker with them off and on. You subscribe to writers magazines, read how-to books, join a writers group and even attend local writers conferences. You enjoy writing and the companionship of writers, but you do not try to sell your material.

Stage Three—Hopeful. Your friends say you are talented. You work diligently on your book for weeks, months or even years until you feel it is perfect. With your heart racing, you send off your first manuscript. You anxiously check the mail. As you tear open the self-addressed 9×12 manila envelope, you envision how you'll spend the advance.

Stage Four—Depression. You receive your first rejection. Then your second, third and fourth. You shout at the absentee editor, or cry, or eat a box of chocolates and commiserate with your writing friends. Every item you send out is rejected, usually with no more than a form letter. Self-doubt soars.

Stage Five—Withdrawal. You convince yourself that you are totally untalented (or that the editors of the world do not appreciate you). You shelve your manuscripts in the attic or garage and tell the rodents to enjoy them. You hate all successful authors, especially R.L. Stine.

Stage Six—Rejuvenation. At the bookstore you notice a young adult (YA) best-seller that's eerily similar to your manuscript. You think that your name could have been on the spine. You dig out all the old dust-covered boxes, renew your subscriptions to writers magazines, join another writers club, attend more conferences, meet writers and editors and take a writing course. This time you set goals.

Stage Seven—Persistence. You set aside time for writing, usually late at night, early in the morning or on weekends. You experiment with techniques and styles until you find the one that feels right. You research the market and send out professional-looking work.

Stage Eight—Breakthrough. You sell your first short piece. It's for a regional publication or a children's magazine and you only receive ten dollars for it, but you celebrate anyway. Rejections still come, but they are personalized, encouraging and do not paralyze you.

Stage Nine—First Big Sale. An editor makes an offer on your young adult novel. One year later, it is published. The future looks rosy.

Stage Ten—Sink or Swim. You sell more articles or maybe even another book. You stash away money until you have enough savings to survive for one year, and then you quit your day job. You write every day and keep several manuscripts in the mail. You are hard-working and dedicated, knowing that if you do not sell, you will have to return to your dreary job.

Stage Eleven—Career Author. Your income derives solely from writing and speaking engagements. As a published author, you are now a business with all the ramifications that it implies. The pressure of meeting deadlines, coping with bad or inaccurate reviews, balancing school visits with research, writing and family, keeping tax records and handling promotion can turn your hair gray. But you keep going; the rewards outweigh the headaches.

Did you recognize yourself in any of these stages? I know I did—every single one. Most of the world's successful authors have gone through similar phases, starting as dreamers, writing on weekends or late at night, and then boldly quitting their jobs and forcing themselves to sell or sink. Rarely does an author become rich and famous overnight. Many children's and YA authors never do, even after thirty books.

Most writers, even the very good ones, go through the first few stages and then give up, or they get stuck in one stage and never move on. One of my friends has been working on the same novel for fifteen years; he has won several contests, but wants the book to be "perfect" before he sends it to a publisher. I've seen others give up after selling one book. I, myself, actually stopped writing for approximately three years after I had two successful adult novels published. It wasn't until I changed from writing adult books to children's books that I found my niche and plowed full steam ahead.

There is nothing wrong with being in Stage Two—writing but never selling. Many people write for their own pleasure with no intention of ever submitting their work to a publisher. Others write for family and friends, and maybe even self-publish.

It takes a very determined person to succeed in the writing business, particularly in the young adult category. This book is intended for those who want to go all the way to Stage Eleven. Part I will discuss the history of the YA category and describe young adult readers. Part II will focus on the various YA categories, including nonfiction, magazines, poetry and picture books. Part III will give advice on setting up your office, setting goals and getting prepared to write. Part IV covers the craft of writing a young adult novel, from character development to plotting to dialogue. And Part V will discuss the business side of writing— studying the market, submitting the manuscript and dealing with rejection, contracts, editors and self-promotion.

No matter what stage of writer's development you are in, hopefully you will find something useful in this book. The YA category is not the easiest one to write for. However, if you are up to a challenge, read on and welcome to the sometimes frustrating, sometimes wonderful and always exciting world of writing for young adults.

PART ONE

The Nature of the Beast

Chapter One

What Is Young Adult Literature?

Writing for young adults is not for the faint of heart. Of all the book categories, young adult (YA) is one of the most unpredictable. Like the characters in the stories and the adolescents who read them, YA literature falls into a space that is not quite children's and not quite adult books. The YA novel bridges childhood and adulthood, and that bridge can be very shaky.

The YA genre embraces many categories—mystery, horror, romance, historical, inspirational, fantasy, science fiction, literary, nonfiction, poetry, short stories and, more recently, picture books. YA novels range from fast-paced, light paperback series to hardcover mainstream literature used by English teachers in the classroom. Virtually every subject known to humankind appears in YA literature. Young adult novels more closely mimic adult novels than any other area of children's publishing, and many are read by adults.

To better understand what the young adult category is about, it is helpful to see where it has been.

THE EARLY YEARS OF YOUNG ADULT LITERATURE

All adults were once young, regardless of the time in which they lived. And every literate person read something during those adolescent years. But throughout most of history, the books read by young adults were the same books read by their elders. Consider Thomas Jefferson, for example. As a young adult, he would have read what was available at the time—the Bible, histories, the works of Shakespeare, Homer, Aristotle, Plato, perhaps some John Donne or Malory, poetry, sonnets, Latin works such as Caesar's *De Bello Gallico*, or books about math, science or architecture. Even if Jefferson had found a book with a teenage protagonist—maybe a young King Arthur drawing the sword from the stone—it is safe to say that such books would have been written *about* young adults, not *for* them.

By the end of the 1800s, some of the world's greatest literature featuring young protagonists had been written—*Alice in Wonderland, Huckleberry Finn, Tom Sawyer, Little Women, Oliver Twist, Great Expectations, Heidi, The Swiss Family Robinson, Treasure Island, Kidnapped* and *The Jungle Book*—but these books were not marketed as young adult literature.

In earlier times, there was a more defined line between children's literature and adult literature, just as there was a more defined line between children and adults. There was no transition period; the word *teenager* was not used in America until after World War II. In the 1800s, a seventeen year old was an adult: Seventeen-year-old "boys" fought in wars and seventeen-year-old "girls" got married and had babies. On farms, thirteen-year-olds were expected to do their share of the work; in large towns, thirteen-year-olds worked in factories. Public schools were not a compulsory institution, and many people, particularly females in rural areas, did not learn to read and write. America was still an agricultural society. A typical one-room school in a small farming community taught only to ninth grade, and many girls did not attend school at all. Adolescents could not be spared from the farm work, and recreational reading was not a part of their lifestyle.

By the 1900s, however, the public school system had been well established, and both male and female children were expected to complete some schooling. As a higher percentage of American children learned to read and write, the need arose for literature aimed directly at students. Some of the great classics were written during the first half of the century—*Rebecca of Sunnybrook Farm, Lad: A Dog, Anne of Green Gables, The Secret Garden, The Yearling, My Friend Flicka* and *Johnny Tremain*, among many others. It seems that any story with an orphaned child or an animal was considered proper reading for American youth. Soon after World War I, the publishing industry established children's literature as a legitimate category of its own.

With America's population booming after World War II, schools were increasingly devoted to separate grade levels—

elementary, junior high and high schools. Busing systems brought farm children into town, and the one-room school vanished. Likewise, the all-knowing one-room school teacher was eventually replaced by teachers trained in specialty fields—history, math, science, English and reading.

By the mid-1950s, when I entered the first grade, children's books had a well-established niche in the publishing industry. There were also several series that appealed to younger teens—Nancy Drew, The Hardy Boys, Trixie Belden, Sue Barton and Cherry Ames—but these books targeted readers ages eight to twelve more than those twelve and up. As a sixth grader, my favorite series was Walter Farley's Black Stallion. The series books were easy to read, fast-paced and squeaky-clean entertainment—the books that boys and girls read for pleasure. They were issued in hardcover rather than paperback, and were usually checked out at the library. The typical adolescent of the 1950s did not have an independent source of income to purchase books.

But what about literature for the classroom? During the 1950s and 1960s, lower grades were dominated by textbooks rather than fiction. The old Dick and Jane books are a prime example. Junior high students had literature printed in anthologies. High school students studied adult literature. I entered seventh grade in 1960, the year Kennedy was elected president and the year John Wayne starred in *The Alamo*. I can remember nearly every book assigned by my teachers from grades nine through twelve and, without exception, not a single one was written for adolescents. Remember *Great Expectations*? What was that all about? It was a miracle teens continued reading at all after struggling through the works of Dickens, Hawthorne, Homer and Thomas Hardy.

Don't misunderstand—I love the classics. But I also remember my friend Margie. An excellent reader, she always had her nose in a book, usually romances or mysteries. She flunked ninth-grade English because she read Cherry Ames books while the teacher lectured about *Great Expectations*. Maybe it was students like Margie who made publishers realize that adolescents deserved books written not just *about* them, but *for* them. Books with characters they could identify with. Books about modern teen problems and woes. Literature that was just as good as that written for adults.

THE TRUE YOUNG ADULT NOVEL IS BORN

The 1960s ushered in the era of the true young adult novel— literature written expressly for teenagers. Some say that the first YA novel was J.D. Salinger's *The Catcher in the Rye*, published in 1951 (although portions of it appeared in magazines as early as 1945). That book certainly created an avalanche of Salinger imitators. However, I find it hard to believe that *Catcher* was written *for* adolescents. None of my friends used that kind of language, and I knew of no one who had read it. I recall my high school English teacher telling us we would not be allowed to read it for class, though she encouraged us to read it on our own. When my mother found a copy hidden under my older brother's pillow, she wept to find that he was reading such "trash." Naturally, I secretly read my brother's collection of Salinger books; but frankly, I didn't understand them and my life was not influenced one way or the other.

Many authorities believe that the YA literature revolution erupted in the late 1960s. In a turbulent social and political climate young adults adopted the war cry "tell it like it is," and authors like S.E. Hinton (a teenager herself) emerged, creating fiction with realistic adolescent characters in realistic situations. Suddenly, young people were no longer portrayed as poor little orphans like Heidi, Rebecca or Anne, whose main concerns were finding love and acceptance. Now the protagonists faced problems such as drugs, violence, sexual abuse, pregnancy, racial prejudice and war. Passage of the civil rights laws and integration of the public school systems created a need for books written about nonwhite cultures. To meet these needs, Asian-, African- and Hispanic-American authors entered the world of young adult literature.

Every problem conceivable became grist for the mill. At last books were being written not only *about* teenagers, but *for* teenagers. And better still, many of the books were literary and meaningful, rather than strictly entertaining. Students loved these books because they addressed contemporary adolescent concerns and were easier to read than the often-dry classics. English teachers loved the books because at last students, even reluctant readers, discovered that reading could be fun. The YA category took off like a rocket.

PAPERBACK YOUNG ADULT NOVELS EMERGE

The YA market continued to flourish during the 1970s, but distribution patterns changed. Traditionally, a children's or young adult book was published in hardcover and sold to the school and library market. If the book received great reviews and was deemed a success, paperback rights were purchased by a company such as Dell, Ballantine or Bantam. Typical paperback markets included drugstores, grocery stores, bookstores and school book clubs. Literary classics were also brought out in paperback to accommodate high school and college English class assignments.

By the 1970s, however, publishers had discovered that modern teens had money of their own and were spending it on paperback books. The trick was to offer them the right kind of books. Teens weren't interested in spending their money on *The Scarlet Letter, The House of the Seven Gables* or hardcover YA novels which often focused on serious teen problems. What these readers wanted were fast-paced, easy-to-read books like the series books of the 1950s, only with contemporary stories and characters.

Publishers rushed in to meet the demand and the paperback series boom of the late 1970s and 1980s was on. The market was flooded with YA series, especially those for girls, and many new publishing imprints or lines sprang up to accommodate the voracious reading appetite of girls ages eleven to thirteen. The romance industry especially experienced a boom, and many adult romance publishers expanded into the YA romance market, hoping to hook young girls on reading romances, developing future customers.

Lines such as Sweet Valley High, Sweet Dreams, Cheerleaders, Wildfire, First Love, Seniors, Sisters and Crosswinds dominated the market. Between 1981 and 1985, the Sweet Dreams series alone sold almost nineteen million books. These books had predictable plots, no serious problems and were squeaky clean—no sex scenes, no profanity and no sad endings. Topics revolved around friendships, cheerleading, being popular and dating. Typical settings included the mall, the prom, high school, sporting events and skating. The protagonists were mostly middle class Euro-Americans. Paperback series brought so much success to the publishers that even hardback publishers entered the paper-back romance market.

Since no one individual could write fast enough to satisfy the reading appetites of the adolescent readers, book packagers emerged to help those publishers who did not want to bother with developing, writing and editing a series. Packagers pro-cured unknown authors and paid them a set fee to ghostwrite formula series books. These books were then released under the name of a known publisher and author. (Book packagers are discussed in chapter three.) Authors with a talent for writing popular paperback fiction earned good incomes in the 1980s.

Of course, with so many publishers jumping on the band-wagon, it was no surprise that the wagon eventually collapsed. By the end of the 1980s, the romance market, both adult and YA, had been inundated. Readers had so many books to choose from that the publishers' profits were spread thin. New lines folded; established lines made cutbacks. I speak of this from personal experience. In 1987, I sold a YA novel to Crosswinds, a new YA imprint. One month before the book's publication date, the company folded. That was typical of the times, as one YA line after another went under.

The market appeared doomed. Compounding the problem was the never-ending cycle of demographics. As one generation of teens outgrew a series, the next generation decided they wanted something different. Series books, like Hula Hoops or beehive hairdos, often follow the patterns of fads or trends. What one generation loves, the next rejects.

During the 1990s, the younger siblings of the romance read-ers, perhaps in rebellion against their older sisters' reading hab-its, focused on something new. This time the rage was horror paperbacks, which took off in the 1990s like the romances of the 1980s. Once again, publishers had hit the mark. Suddenly boys became avid readers, too, even though boys had tradition-ally been categorized as nonreaders by the time they reached seventh grade.

For YA horror fans, there were books by Christopher Pike and series like Fear Street by R.L. Stine. Preteen readers sank their teeth into Stine's Goosebumps series, a modern-day pub-lishing phenomenon that demonstrates how marketing and product merchandising can influence young readers. Collecting the books, as well as related merchandise, became a fad. Scholastic's two middle-grade series, Baby-Sitters Club and Goosebumps, dominated the market and generated millions of dollars in profit. But like all fads, horror, too, had a limited life expectancy. By the end of the 1990s, Goosebumps sales dropped off, and Scholastic had to make cutbacks and layoffs.

YOUNG ADULT HARDCOVER LITERATURE

The collapse of the Goosebumps empire demonstrates the risk of writing for trends. Many authors, on seeing the success of horror novels, quickly wrote horror into their plots, only to find that by the time the manuscript was finished, the market was gone. Other popular trends of the 1990s included environmental issues, homelessness and AIDS.

Trends may come and go, but the YA market will always have room for serious, hardcover literature. YA authors such as Katherine Paterson, Robert Cormier, Richard Peck, Walter Dean Myers, Cynthia Voigt and Virginia Hamilton will always have a place with young adult readers. Consistent good writing about varied topics is the trademark of these writers. Often, these are the books assigned by English teachers, the books that appear on school or library recommended reading lists. These are the books that receive good reviews, awards and honors. These, too, are the books that will exist long after the series books are gone.

Chapter Two

Writers and Readers of Young Adult Literature

Before dipping your toes into the turbulent waters of writing for young adults, there are several questions to consider.

WHY WRITE FOR YOUNG ADULTS?

Some uninformed observers may assume that writing for young adults is easier than writing for adults, and that this market can be used as a testing ground or as a stepping stone for authors who eventually want to write more difficult, more meaningful adult literature. Nothing could be further from the truth. Writing for younger readers entails unique challenges and responsibilities. I wrote for adults before switching to writing for children and teens. I made the change because I found writing for young people more rewarding.

In writing a YA novel or nonfiction book, you will use the same writing techniques as a writer of adult literature. However, there are obvious differences. Your style will be more straightforward and direct, with fewer words to convey the story. Your protagonist will be younger, and the focus of the subject matter will be different. Ernest Hemingway wrote about war from the perspective of adults; Walter Dean Myers wrote about war from the perspective of eighteen and nineteen year olds.

Writing for young adults also often means having greater influence on your reader. An adult reader has set philosophies and views and is not often persuaded to change them by reading a novel. But a young adult, who is tenderhearted and inexperienced in life, can be profoundly changed by the words in a book—as I have learned from many of the fan letters I receive each year. For this reason, the author of children's and young adult literature

must take more responsibility for what goes into a book.

There are three basic reasons to write: to entertain, to inform or to stimulate intellectual activity. The most memorable works combine aspects of all three. A truly good nonfiction book is presented in an entertaining, compelling way so that the reader does not realize he is actually learning something. And likewise, a great YA novel teaches the reader and causes him to think without interfering with the story. And isn't intellectual activity, such as the thoughts stimulated by reading a good poem, really a form of entertainment?

You may find that your strength lies in nonfiction, or that you prefer short stories or poetry to the novel. But whether you decide to write a lengthy, educational opus or a fast-paced, entertaining story, you must have respect for the young adult reader and a basic understanding of what adolescents are going through.

WHO WRITES FOR YOUNG ADULTS?

Authors who write for children and young adults are among the best-educated authors of any category and often have an innate propensity for imparting knowledge to others. Perhaps you are a teacher, a librarian or a professional in the education field. Maybe you work with adolescents on either a professional or a voluntary basis. Or maybe you are the parent of teenagers. You don't have to love teenagers—there are times when we all feel that adolescents are the most self-centered, uncontrollable creatures on earth—but you must be able to realistically and honestly portray their point of view in your writing, and you must be able to respect their problems and concerns.

As I travel around the country speaking to schoolchildren, librarians, teachers and writers, people often seem amazed to learn that I do not have children. Being a parent is not a prerequisite for writing good YA books, no more than being a parent is a requirement for being a good teacher. What is necessary is the ability to remember what it was like to be young, and the ability to put yourself in the shoes of a young protagonist. I've often said that writers have split personalities and are frustrated actors at heart, because when you are writing fiction you must act out the roles of all of your characters.

HOW OLD ARE YOUNG ADULT READERS?

I remember the first time I saw the words *young adult*. It was 1960 and our family had moved to a very small farming town. On our first day at a new church I saw those dubious words on the door of a Sunday school classroom. My brothers and I stood in the hall debating. In our eyes, a "young adult" was just that, an adult who was still young, say twenty or so. That meant someone who was no longer a teen, someone who held down a job and definitely had already graduated from high school. I, a lowly twelve year old, did not dream of going in. Eventually my brothers, ages sixteen and eighteen, stepped inside the classroom with trepidation.

Two years later, when we moved to a larger town, the situation was repeated. This time I entered the young adult classroom and was surrounded mostly by other ninth-grade students and a sprinkling of totally bored and disinterested high school students. The term young adult, it seems, was more or less synonymous with teenager.

Thirty-five years later, as an author of YA literature, most of my fan letters come from readers ages eleven and twelve. Occasionally a ten year old writes, often with an accompanying photo of a sweet smiling face, telling me how much she enjoyed my YA novels such as *Indio*. I must say I cringe when I think of a ten year old reading scenes of sexual abuse, death and suffering. But such is the nature of the beast called *YA literature*. The readers get younger and younger.

Ask ten people today to define a young adult reader and you are likely to get ten different answers, according to their own personal experiences. Traditionally, YA has been defined as ages twelve and up. However, some publishers have subdivided the category into "young YA" and "older YA." To add to the confusion, there is much overlapping among these subcategories. A mature sixth grader, age eleven, might read and understand books aimed at ninth graders. On the other hand, a reluctant eighth-grade reader may have a difficult time reading a novel aimed at fifth graders.

"Young" YA literature is generally read by those in grades five through seven (ages ten through thirteen). "Older" YA is typically read by those in grades eight and nine (ages thirteen through fifteen). Rarely do high school students above tenth grade read YA literature, with the possible exception of YA mysteries, such as those written by Joan Lowery Nixon, and some of the more mature YA romances. Teenagers over fifteen read adult literature as English class assignments, or they read adult novels, nonfiction and magazines for pleasure. I have visited hundreds of schools across the country and the world, yet only twice have I spoken to high school students in grades ten through twelve, and in both cases those were gifted and talented students interested in learning how to write.

Another important fact to keep in mind is that young readers prefer to read about a protagonist a bit older than they are. An eleven year old will read about a thirteen or fourteen year old; a fourteen year old will read about a sixteen or seventeen year old; and older high school students read about adult characters in their twenties (or older). There are exceptions, but generally speaking, when you write young adult literature today, you are writing for middle school and junior high students.

WHAT MAKES TODAY'S READERS TICK?

Psychologists are quick to point out numerous facts:

- 50 percent of all marriages today end in divorce, so virtually all American adolescents either have divorced parents or have friends with divorced parents
- adolescents read less today because of distractions such as TV, video games and recreational and school activities
- today's adolescents are highly visual
- today's adolescents have a shorter attention span and want quick gratification
- adolescents are exposed to drugs, sex, profanity and violence on TV, in movies and in the schools more than any previous generation
- girls reach puberty at a younger age today
- more teens are sexually active and are having babies in junior high, and even in middle school in some cases
- today's adolescents spend more money than any previous generation
- reading scores on national tests are lower
- today's schools are a mixture of many different races

- violence on school campuses is greater than it was twenty-five years ago

If you have not been inside a junior high or high school lately, you are probably in for a shock. But before you write off today's teens as alien creatures or a lost cause, remember that they are no less intelligent, no less cognitive, nor less valuable human beings than adults. They are simply younger and have had fewer life experiences to draw from before making critical decisions. Naturally, at times their actions will look awkward or impertinent.

WHAT DO THE STATISTICS MEAN TO THE WRITER?

The statistics mean that you will probably not write another *Rebecca of Sunnybrook Farm* or *Anne of Green Gables*, but this does not mean that you should feel that you cannot write for young adult readers.

Let me make a confession: I never attended a high school dance, not even the prom. I never dated in high school. I hated cheerleaders and never wanted to be one. I didn't get a car until I was twenty. I never owned a stereo or bought records. I think teenagers can be the most annoying, selfish people on earth. I hate malls. Older teenagers scare me.

So, how can I possibly be an author of YA novels? I simply acknowledge that today's readers are different in many ways and face problems that I never did, but I also know that some things never change.

I do not try to write about modern adolescents per se. I write about the universal, never-changing human adolescent that has existed for thousands of years in many cultures. I remember what it felt like to be a teenager: the pain of being unpopular and insecure, having crushes on inaccessible boys, hating snooty girls, being too tall, too skinny, too poor and too ugly. And deep inside, every teenager, whether packing a gun in a dark alley or popping gum at a mall, whether fighting in the American Revolution or sweating in the rice fields of Vietnam, feels the same emotions that I felt. The clothes, the cars, the language, the customs and even the moral values may differ, but inside those beasts called young adults still beats the human heart.

If you cannot remember your adolescence and cannot love your adolescent protagonist, chances are you will not be happy writing for young adults. But, if the memory of that first kiss makes you smile, if the memory of that first heartache makes you sigh and if the memory of that big embarrassing moment makes you wince, then are you ready to plunge into the chilly, dark waters and discover the wondrous treasure that comes with writing for young adults. But before you begin, you need to know what kinds of young adult literature are being written today.

PART TWO

What's On the Young Adult Shelf

Chapter Three

Dark and Dreary or Light and Airy? Young Adult Genre Fiction

Like adult fiction, young adult fiction covers a broad spectrum of topics and categories. So vast is the range that it will take four chapters to discuss all categories—novels, shorter works (poetry, short stories and picture books) and nonfiction. I will begin with YA novels, because that is what people most often think of when they hear the words *young adult book*.

YOUNG ADULT GENRE FICTION

The term *genre* derives from the Latin word *genus*, which means race or kind. In the publishing industry, *genre* refers to books that have certain traits in common. Categorizing books into genres is a quick way of letting readers know what the book is about. If you love mysteries, you go to the mystery section of the bookstore, knowing that all books in that genre will contain a crime to be solved.

Young adult fiction uses the same genres as adult fiction: mystery, romance, historical, adventure/survival, inspirational, horror and science fiction/fantasy. Many stories are mixed genres. For example, a science fiction protagonist may travel back in time to a historical event; a romance heroine may solve a murder mystery; an inspirational novel may involve a life and death survival. (Those books that do not fall into a specific genre are called *general, mainstream* or *literary fiction* and will be discussed in the next chapter.)

Here is a quick review of what elements belong to each genre.

Mysteries

One of the most consistently popular genres for children, young adults and adults is the mystery novel. The YA mystery uses the same writing techniques as an adult mystery novel, and indeed many adults read YA mysteries. The primary differences between adult and YA mysteries are (1) the protagonist will be a teenager, (2) there will be no explicit sex scenes, and (3) there will be no graphic scenes of violence.

The mystery for older YA readers usually involves a murder, but for younger readers, ages ten to twelve, the mystery might revolve around a kidnapping, a theft or a missing child. In addition to the main mystery that will be solved, the protagonist should also have a personal problem. Perhaps the heroine is homeless or lost in a foreign land; perhaps she feels inferior to an older sibling or has suffered through the recent divorce of her parents. The personal problem will help the readers identify with the protagonist. Its resolution will come as a result of solving the main mystery, which the protagonist should accomplish herself, rather than by accident or by adult intervention.

Since young readers tend to be impatient, it is important to introduce the protagonist, the personal problem and the mystery early in the story. A good mystery will also have subplots, or mini-mysteries, occurring and being solved throughout the story. Since the main mystery will not be solved until the end of the book, it is important to include clues throughout the story. But do not wait until the last minute to mention a critical person or clue. False clues (red herrings) make the story more interesting, but do not just stick the clues and red herrings anywhere you please. They must be logical, explainable and an integral part of the story.

Tension can be created by a feeling of impending danger, and also by imposing time limits on the protagonist. For example, if the heroine does not complete a certain task or solve a certain clue by midnight, her kidnapped baby sister will be killed, or a bomb will blow up the gymnasium at a basketball game. To create a sense of pacing, however, alternate each scene that is filled with action and tension with a scene that is slower paced and reflective.

As with any novel, the hero will have goals and encounter obstacles. In this case the goal will be to solve the mystery and the personal problem. Obstacles will be thrown out by the villain and false clues will take the hero temporarily down the wrong path. Because the hero is human, he will fail from time to time, come to wrong conclusions, get into trouble and, often, lose ground. Each time an obstacle is overcome, the hero will face another one even greater than the last. When one suspect is eliminated, another pops up. Throwing suspicion on many people increases the suspense. The ripple effect helps to tie the plot together. Something that the protagonist does in chapter one affects something in chapter two, which affects chapter three and so on.

The tension increases until the final climax, in which the last obstacle is the greatest (often life-threatening) and seems unsurpassable. The climax is the highest point of tension. The action is faster, the sentences shorter and the emotions greater. After the climax comes the resolution of the personal problem, the explanation of any loose ends and a satisfying ending that implies hope.

A thriller is much like a mystery, but usually has more violence and more fear. There may be more than one death, and the protagonist is in greater jeopardy. Think of the movie *Psycho*, and you have the makings of a thriller.

Horror and the Supernatural

In horror novels, the threat of death is more violent and intense than in a mystery. Rarely is just one person killed. And people are not just being killed, people are being horribly mutilated—beheaded, axed or disemboweled. The murderer is not a sly intellectual or a calculating criminal, but a demented madman who kills for pleasure, is at times irrational and hides in cellars and basements. He may even be a nonhuman being—monster, ghost, alien or ghoul. In horror novels, the physical threat to the hero and his friends is far greater. The element of surprise is used more extensively, creating more sudden fear in the reader. Readers of horror want to feel the adrenaline flowing, feel the increased heartbeat and feel the fear of being suddenly frightened.

As in the mystery, the tension and fear gradually increase with each chapter. Often the protagonist's friends are picked off one by one, and no one is above suspicion. The final climax is very intense, and the madman is usually dealt a demise befitting his own acts. For examples of YA horror, read the works of Christopher Pike and R.L. Stine.

Not all supernatural stories are horror stories with intense violence. In Gothic ghost stories the skies are dark and dreary, it rains a lot and the protagonist is typically an orphaned heroine who must work in a large, dark house with strange, mysterious people, as well as ghosts of the past. In the Gothic story, the mystery frequently centers on why the dead person's spirit became a ghost (often an unpunished crime) and how to resolve the problem so that the spirit can rest in peace. Of course, some ghost stories are set in modern times. An excellent example of this kind of story for ages eight through twelve is *Time for Andrew: A Ghost Story* by Mary Downing Hahn. My own ghost story, *Cabin 102*, alternates between a modern-day teenager on a cruise ship in the Caribbean and the ghost of an Arawak Indian girl whose spirit becomes trapped on a Spanish galleon during a hurricane in the year 1511. In both of these examples, the ghosts are friendly and nonthreatening to the hero.

Romance

Although the heyday of the YA series romance has passed, adolescent girls still want love stories. Girls (boys are interested, too, but most will not admit it) are curious about the opposite sex and sex itself, as well as about dating, that first kiss or dance, and all the social customs. These readers want to know what to do, and seek comfort in romances that depict girls in situations similar to their own. Young romance readers fall into three age categories: eight through twelve (middle-grade readers); ten through thirteen (young YA); and twelve and up (older YA). By high school, older teens are reading adult romances.

For younger romance readers, ages ten to twelve, the books often feature clubs with several female characters. The protagonists in these books attend junior high, and their social lives often revolve around a mutual activity such as horseback riding, ice-skating, ballet or sports. Romance in the lower YA fiction means a boy-girl relationship without sex, and often it means first love.

For the young YA readers ages ten through thirteen, series such as Sweet Valley High and Class Secrets have high school settings. The plots are fast-paced, romance is the focus of the stories, and the settings are the high school, the classroom, and outside activities such as sports events, concerts and the beach.

For older YA readers, series with university-age girls, such as Sweet Valley University and Freshman Dorm, are a bit more realistic. The protagonists face the problems of college life, friendships, love and sex in the 1990s. The point of view may even shift among several primary characters, including the males. Such romances may appear as single-title paperbacks, trilogies or miniseries of five books written by the same author. Love scenes are more sensual than the sweet romances of the past or the romances for younger readers. Historical YA romances also have been increasing in popularity. These are usually single-title releases and are much longer than other YA genre novels.

Conflict in YA romances can be created by such devices as competition from another girl, misunderstandings, differences in beliefs or politics, socioeconomic barriers, distance, age or parental interference.

Remember that young readers want to read about characters slightly older than they are. In junior high or high school, just one grade level can make a difference in peer approval. If you are writing a teen romance for girls ages ten through thirteen, the heroine should be at least fourteen. The hero should be the same age as, or a year or two older than, the heroine. However, having a mature man court a teenage girl is a no-no.

Speaking of no-no's, although the topics of today's YA romances may be more mature than in the past, taboos still exist. *Romance* does not mean explicit sex. Far more important than graphic sex scenes are the underlying emotions of the boy-girl relationship—the jubilant joy of being together, the excruciating pain of separation, the insecurity, the fear of rejection, the conflict and tension, and the triumph of that first love.

As for profanity, although some mainstream YA novels allow it, the YA romance series does not. If the plot requires profanity, whether from shock or anger, I prefer to use description rather than speech. For example, "He spewed out a string of curse words that shriveled my toes," gets the point across.

YA romances usually require happy, or at least hopeful, endings. In either case, the protagonist should grow. She should learn something from the experience that has transpired for the past 45,000 words. She learns something about herself, about love and relations or about life. After finishing a YA romance, the reader should put it down not with a feeling of "the end," but rather with the feeling of "the beginning."

Fantasy/Science Fiction

It is safe to say that fantasy authors live in a world of their own. One of the characteristics of fantasy and science fiction is the creation of nonexisting worlds. Many authors consider these the most difficult types of novels to write because of the sheer amount of imagination that goes into creating a whole new world. Some of the most famous literature is classified as fantasy: *Alice in Wonderland, The Wizard of Oz, The Wind in the Willows, Charlotte's Web, Watership Down, A Wrinkle in Time, A Connecticut Yankee in King Arthur's Court* and *The Indian in the Cupboard.* The common thread in all of these is, as renowned fantasy author Jane Yolen says, "the suspension of disbelief." In other words, anything goes as long as the author says so.

There are three basic types of fantasy: (1) animal fantasies, (2) normal humans thrust into fantasy worlds, and (3) fantasy worlds. In the first category, which includes stories such as *Charlotte's Web, Stuart Little, The Tale of Peter Rabbit* and *The Wind in the Willows,* the animals talk and play and work and have lives here on planet Earth. In the second category, the human visitors—Alice sliding down the rabbit hole, Dorothy carried by a tornado to Oz or Gulliver being toted by Lilliputians—are strangers in fantastic lands with talking animals, sorcerers and all sorts of lovely creatures. In the last category, set in imaginary lands or an Earth of long ago or in the future, everyone in the fantasy lives in that world; Earth as we know it today does not exist. *The Hobbit* and *The Lord of the Rings* fall into this category, and many readers, when they say *fantasy,* have these in mind.

In fantasy, the imaginary world often centers on mythological stories, famous legends or fairy tales. Common themes include the quest of a young, innocent person (often aided by a wise man or wizard), or a hero who must face multiheaded beasts to save his land or his love. Fantasies portray the never-ending struggle of good against evil. Those who are good are pure of heart and soul, honorable and valiant; those who are evil are wicked to the bone. Protagonists are often put to the test, progressing through stages in a world populated with elves, dragons, gnomes, ghosts, oracles, wizards, sorcerers, fairies and talking animals. But the hero must win the battle himself, for kingdoms and entire worlds are at stake. *The Odyssey* was one of the first great fantasies.

Though the created fantasy world exists only in the mind of the author and the reader, rules of that universe must apply consistently throughout the book, just as surely as the laws of physics must apply here on Earth. If water runs upstream on page 3, it must run upstream on page 300, too. As Yolen says: "Logic must be the most important element in a fantasy book."

Perhaps more than in other genres, strong visual descriptions are essential, since the author speaks of a world that the readers have not seen before. The landscapes, laws, religions and customs—all the features of the world—must be clear. The same goes for the nonhuman creatures that inhabit these magical worlds: Their characters must be fully developed, because the reader has no previous creatures for reference. Perhaps this is one reason that many fantasies tend to run a bit longer than contemporary novels. But like any good novel, too much description can bog the story down. The basic rule of *show, don't tell* is just as critical in fantasy as elsewhere. Character should be revealed through action and reaction, rather than by lengthy passages of description.

Fantasies often utilize symbolism, profound philosophies and poetic language. Kings use words from the days of yore; poetic devices such as alliteration and metaphor abound. Fantasies dramatically stir strong emotions in the reader, allowing the expression of values that in other categories might appear foolish and melodramatic—hope, truth, honor, love, loyalty, courage, evil and purity. For fine examples of fantasy, read the works of Anne McCaffrey, Ursula Le Guin, Madeleine L'Engle and Jane Yolen.

Closely associated with fantasy is the futuristic and science fiction category. *Futuristic* often implies planet Earth, but with a time setting in the future. The Newbery Award-winning novel *The Giver*, by Lois Lowry, is an example of a futuristic novel. Like fantasy, future worlds have set rules that must be obeyed. The purpose of these books is often to comment on some aspect of today's society.

Science fiction often implies a setting of another planet or universe, and involves technical jargon and explanations of spaceships, space stations and phenomena of outer space. Again, a whole new world with laws, social rules and consistent logic is created.

Historical

These are my favorite young adult books to write. I love to research the past, to discover how historical events affected the lives of ordinary people and helped shape the world as we know it today. In many ways, historicals are the opposite of fantasies. Instead of worlds where everything is created anew, historical novels present worlds in which every detail, from the description of the hero's belt buckle to the kind of lamp used to light the room, actually existed.

The popularity of historical novels has waxed and waned. They sank from a peak of popularity in the 1950s to a valley of despair in the 1970s, and then rebounded in the 1980s. It has often been said that teenagers of today do not care about the past because they are too self-centered to find its relevancy. But recently, more teens seem interested in reading about the past. Historical romances are gaining favor with girls.

And, for the eight through twelve age group, historical series are popular. The Orphan Train series has been successful for years. The introduction in 1986 of the American Girl series astounded the publishing industry. Between 1986 and 1996, this phenomenal series sold over thirty-nine million books in addition to millions of dollars worth of associated merchandise such as dolls and coloring books.

In 1996, Scholastic introduced its Dear America series, with each book depicting a famous event in American history told in the format of a girl's diary. These hardcover books hit the bestseller list the month they were released. Harper released a historical series based on the ancestors of Laura Ingalls Wilder. Several other publishers have also issued new historical imprints targeted at girls. For examples of excellent YA historical fiction, read Ann Rinaldi, Kristiana Gregory, Scott O'Dell and Carolyn Meyer.

Today's students and teachers demand more accuracy than in past years, especially in the area of depicting minority cultures. Native Americans are no longer seen as massacring savages, nor are slaves portrayed as uneducated and submissive. More than any other category, historicals demand extensive research. The author must learn about every aspect of the characters' daily lives during the set time period—clothing, food, language, transportation, communication, songs, dances, habitats, occupations, religion, taboos, laws, politics, education, toys and current events in the rest of the world.

It is difficult to complete a historical novel in less than one year. Writing a historical requires a lot of curiosity, patience and perseverance. You must be willing to dig through countless books, magazine articles, archives of old diaries and letters. It's no coincidence that many authors of historicals also enjoy hobbies such as genealogy research and putting together puzzles.

One pitfall of writing a historical novel is the temptation to never stop the research. Considering that there are university professors who have spent their entire lives studying one tiny period of history, it is safe to say that you will never learn everything there is to know in a year's time. Accept this and move on with the story and characters. Your job is to create the feel of the time period and report events accurately, but more importantly, you must tell a good story with believable characters. Young adult readers want to be swept up in the pain of war, the agony of childbirth or the cruelty of slavery. They do not want to get bogged down with too many details.

There are two basic types of historical fiction: fiction based on true historical events and fiction set during a specific historical period. In the first type, the plot will incorporate actual events, such as famous battles, famous human catastrophes, natural disasters, inventions and so forth. Historical personages often make cameo appearances, or even play major roles in the plot. Examples of this kind of fiction are Kristiana Gregory's *Earthquake at Dawn* (the San Francisco earthquake), Scott O'Dell's *Sing Down the Moon* (the relocation of Native Americans in the southwest to reservations), Isabelle Holland's *Behind the Lines* (the New York Draft Riots during the Civil War) and my novel *A Line in the Sand* (Texas War of Independence and the Battle of the Alamo).

In the second type of historical novel, no major historical event takes place; rather, a feeling of the time period is created through accurate descriptions, dialogue, clothing and situations that could have happened. Examples of this kind of fiction include Avi's *The True Confessions of Charlotte Doyle* (set in the 1800s), Karen Cushman's novel *Catherine Called Birdy* (set in the middle ages) and my novel *Indio* (set in the 1500s).

Anachronisms, the use of items or words that were not in use at the time, are a common error in historical fiction. Though it is not desirable to have the characters speak exactly as they did in the past, avoid using modern speech patterns and slang. Someone from the 1940s might say "swell" but not "groovy." Before using any slang word, consult a dictionary of slang to verify if it was used during that time period. A sprinkling of archaic words helps to create the dialogue of the past. A *thou, thee, thy, thine* or *'tis* creates the feeling of colonial Puritans. One of the best ways to get an accurate feel for language is to read journals and letters or works of literature written during the time period. For more recent history, such as the 1930s or 1940s, watch old black and white movies or listen to old radio programs. (See chapter nine for a discussion on historical fiction research resources.)

As in any good novel, the central character should have personal goals and problems in addition to the historical backdrop for the story. For example, in my YA historical *The Last Rainmaker*, which is set in 1900, the backdrop is the Wild West shows that traveled across America displaying American Indians, cowboys and other symbols of the vanishing American frontier. The personal problem of the heroine, Caroline, supersedes the backdrop. She has run away from home and joined the Wild West show in hopes of finding out who her mother was, a woman who died after giving birth and whose heritage has been withheld from Caroline all her life. The mystery of her mother's identity and life is the driving force for Caroline, but along the way the reader learns about traveling shows, the treatment of Indians, the demise of buffalo and many other aspects of the changing American West.

Another important point to remember is that history to today's adolescent readers does not necessarily mean the 1800s or earlier. To today's youth, the 1950s or the Vietnam War is history. Even if you lived during those time periods, there is research to do. Go through old newspapers or magazines, or watch old news reels, to refresh your memories.

The history you choose to write about may be as dramatic as the Battle of Gettysburg or as quiet as a Quaker village, but always remember that history is only the backdrop. For fiction, don't let the historical event become the only focus of the book. The character and the character's story are what will keep the reader turning the pages.

Inspirational

Like romances, inspirational books are most often read by girls. The heroine is an ordinary girl who is suddenly faced with a faith-challenging situation such as her own illness or the illness of a loved one. She is typically sweet and of strong moral character, and in the end she triumphs over her situation by turning to her faith. But the stories are not preachy; any religious messages are subtle. These books are usually short and emotionally charged. The heroine (or her parent, sibling or friend) may even die. Girls reading these books may cry buckets of tears. But in the end, there is an uplifting sense of triumph, hope and inspiration. For examples of these books, read anything written by Lurlene McDaniels, the self-admitted "queen of the teen tearjerkers," or inspirational novels by Janette Oke.

Adventure/Survival

The adventure story pits the hero or heroine against the forces of nature or unsavory bad guys—a storm at sea, a wild animal or a criminal hunting the protagonist down. Many of the stories involve a journey to an unfamiliar, and sometimes exotic, environment. But the adventure itself is not enough to carry the story. The protagonist must also have personal demons to wrestle with. The adventure story has lots of action and is fast-paced. The hero gets into deeper and deeper trouble as the story progresses until it becomes a matter of life and death. Though extraordinary things happen to the protagonists, the events must be believable and logical. This genre is especially popular with boys.

Closely associated with the adventure story is the survival story. A survival story implies jeopardy and a life-threatening situation, but not necessarily as much action as in an adventure. A survival story can take place within the confines of one locale—a boy alone in the woods (*Hatchet* by Gary Paulsen), a girl alone on an island (*Island of the Blue Dolphins* by Scott O'Dell) or a girl living with wolves (*Julie of the Wolves* by Jean Craighead George). Survival stories are enjoyed by both boys and girls.

WHAT IS YOUNG ADULT SERIES FICTION?

A discussion of genre fiction naturally leads to a discussion of YA series, since most series fall into a specific genre. Many people use the terms *genre fiction* and *paperback series* interchangeably. This implies that any genre book is a fast-paced, light series book. Nothing could be farther from the truth. *Lonesome Dove*, a western, won the Pulitzer Prize; *The Giver*, a futuristic novel, won the Newbery Award, as did *A Wrinkle in Time*, a science fiction novel. These books were all published in hardcover, have distinctive literary styles and are discussed in English classes along with literary classics. To avoid confusion, I will use the term *paperback series* rather than *genre fiction* when referring to the fast-paced YA novels that readers so quickly consume.

Mention YA novels, and most people conjure up the image of row after row of YA series paperbacks lining the bookstore shelves—romances, mysteries, horror and fantasy. Many times these books are released under the name of one author (even though many authors ghostwrite them) and are arranged by series number. Typically they are fast-paced, light reading whose primary purpose is escapist entertainment. In this category, paperbacks reign supreme and the length tends to be shorter than mainstream novels, averaging around 40,000 words.

Series books are often selected and purchased by young readers at retail distributors such as bookstores, drugstores and grocery stores, and through book clubs. Although topics and trends come and go, series paperback books remain read more than any other category, and some popular series sell well into the millions.

WHERE DO BOOK PACKAGERS FIT IN?

Although some series are still developed and produced directly by the publisher, today many of the most successful series are handled by book packagers. In the 1970s, when paperback series books began to catch on like wildfire, it became obvious that no single author could write fast enough to satisfy the appetites of the young readers, mostly girls ages nine through thirteen. And since each story had the same characters, same setting, same writing style and similar plots, any good author could, in theory, write one of the novels. It was assumed that the young readers would not know the difference.

Book packagers came into existence to help publishers solve the problem of producing many books in a short period of time. The packagers often create the series themselves and present the idea to a major paperback publisher such as Bantam. If the deal is made, the packager then locates authors and usually handles the editing. When the series is released, the books will have the publisher's imprint and one author's name on the covers, though many authors wrote them. Occasionally, an established author creates a series and writes the first few books and then turns the subsequent books over to a packager. In this case, the original author gets a percentage of the royalties.

Most often, the author of the packaged book is paid a flat rate or a one-time fee. Some call this a work-for-hire situation. The average payment for a flat-fee packaged novel is between three and five thousand dollars. Most of the time the author does not receive royalties on the book, no matter how many millions of copies it may sell, and the author does not get his or her name on the book cover. However, occasionally the author is allowed to use his or her name and does receive royalties. These are often single-title books or miniseries of three to five books. These books have usually been originated by the author and proposed to the packager.

Book packaging companies are open to hiring beginning authors. The author first queries the packager, providing writing credentials and often writing samples. The packager will then send the author "the bible" for a certain series. This thick packet of information gives the guidelines for the series, including traits of the characters, background material and so forth. After reading the guidelines and several of the books already published in the series, the prospective author will send sample chapters of his manuscript to the packager. If the packager decides to hire the author, he will be sent a contract and a due date. One of the most critical aspects of writing for packagers is the ability to write quickly and consistently. A typical YA series novel is written in one or two months. There is no room for missed deadlines or sitting around waiting for creative genius to take you by the hand.

The first major packagers were Jeff and Dan Weiss, who formed Cloverdale Press, a company which specialized in romances for adults and young adults. Later, Dan Weiss formed his own company, Dan Weiss and Associates. Other large packagers include Mega-Books and Parachute Press. The Society of Children's Book Writers and Illustrators provides an extensive list of book packagers to its members free of charge. (See Appendix for address.)

WRITING SERIES FICTION

If you want to write series fiction, you should first read several successful series to get a feel for the kind of writing expected of the author. Three popular series are Fear Street by R.L. Stine (horror), Nancy Drew by Carolyn Keene (mystery) and Sweet Valley High by Francine Pascal (romance).

When writing series fiction, whether packaged or not, the writer should keep several things in mind. Because of TV and movies, today's readers are highly visual. They are used to things happening at the flip of a switch. They have little patience for long stretches of description. They want to be plunged into the action immediately.

Today's readers come from many different ethnic cultures. YA novels should reflect the cultural diversity of schools, especially those with urban settings. This includes not only students, but teachers and administrators as well. Stereotyping is not acceptable and cultural accuracy is crucial. (See chapter six for a discussion on multicultural literature.)

Series YA fiction tends to be more conservative and less risk-taking than nonseries YA fiction. Controversial issues such as incest, homosexual relationships, profanity, teen pregnancy or graphic sex rarely appear in YA series books because the publishers are trying to appeal to a broader readership or to the masses. Here are a few pointers to keep in mind when writing series YA fiction.

1. Open with a hook—action, a problem or a change—and get into the story immediately.

2. End each chapter with a "catch" or "cliff-hanger" to make the reader want to continue.
3. Make dialogue believable, but avoid contemporary slang that may be out of date by the time your book is published. Avoid profanity.
4. Quicken the pace by avoiding excessive description and overuse of dialogue. Replace adjectives and adverbs with strong, descriptive verbs.
5. Avoid lengthy flashbacks that slow the action. Reveal background material in dialogue and short flashbacks.
6. Use sensory perception—the five senses.
7. Don't preach. Moral lessons should be subtle and shown rather than told.
8. Let the protagonists solve their own problems, rather than having an adult do it for them.
9. Do not include explicit sex scenes, even in YA romances.
10. Make the protagonist slightly older than the intended reading audience.

Writing for a series can be fun and lucrative. I know authors who make a good living writing nothing but packaged paperback series. But writing for a series is not for everyone. If you long to see your name in print, like to take time creating your own plots and characters, and want your book to be released in hardcover and remain on the shelves for many years, you will most likely want to write a nonseries books. These books are often more challenging to write, but the rewards are worthwhile.

Chapter Four

Nonseries Young Adult Literature

A lthough there are rows and rows of series books on the shelves in bookstores, it is difficult to become the author of a successful series. For most authors, the form of writing most often chosen is one that does not neatly fall into a specific genre. This broad category includes hardcover fiction, original paperbacks, poetry anthologies, short stories and YA picture books.

HARDCOVER YOUNG ADULT FICTION

Teenagers will spend their own money on paperback series novels, but rarely will they lay out fifteen dollars or so to buy a hardcover YA novel. As a result, the market for hardcover young adult literature has traditionally been limited to schools and libraries. In the 1980s, the market received a substantial boost when schools began using the whole language teaching method. In the whole language approach, teachers use not only textbooks, but also related literature, to teach a subject. For example, history teachers might assign *The Red Badge of Courage* while studying the Civil War, or Walter Dean Myers's *Fallen Angels* while studying the Vietnam War.

This new teaching method created a demand for literature that could be tied in with curriculums for all grade levels. Suddenly, the hardcover market flourished. Some of the best YA literature—such as the works of Katherine Paterson, Cynthia Voight, Cynthia Ryland, Virginia Hamilton, Paula Fox, Gary Paulsen, Robert Cormier and Richard Peck—was written during this period. Unfortunately, during the 1990s, many school districts across the United States experienced budget cutbacks. Library funds were among the first to suffer. As city and state government cutbacks continued, the amount of YA hardcover literature being published was markedly curtailed. There is still, however, a small, steady market for good literature, and probably always will be. If funds return to schools, another wave of growth will surely follow.

MAINSTREAM FICTION VS. SERIES FICTION

Young adult mainstream fiction differs from series fiction in many aspects. The most obvious difference is the binding process: Series fiction is initially released in paperback and is rarely converted to hardcover; mainstream fiction is first released in hardcover and then in paperback about a year later, if it proves to be successful.

With their own money, young readers purchase paperback series from mass market outlets (grocery, drug and discount stores), and also from bookstores, book clubs and school book fairs. Hardback YA literature, on the other hand, is purchased primarily by institutions, such as libraries and schools, or by adults. Institutions usually purchase the books through discount book jobbers or directly from the publisher. Parents find a very small selection of hardcover YA literature in bookstores; only a few titles are distributed through book clubs and book fairs. Paperback series books do not receive reviews from major review journals; YA literature does. Paperback series have reasonably low prices; hardcover YA books are more expensive.

The most important difference between series paperbacks and YA mainstream literature is the purpose behind each. Like series paperbacks, YA mainstream literature entertains and tells a good story (all good novels must do that), but it also has something important to say. Young adult mainstream literature informs, educates and stimulates intellectual activity. It encourages the young reader to think—about life, love, other cultures, war, religion or racism—and yet does so without being didactic. This is not to say that series fiction does not stimulate its readers, but mainstream fiction does so to a deeper and more profound degree. The fact that YA literature is sold in hardcover implies a faith by the publishers that the book will remain in print for many years.

A literary novel may have elements of a genre book—it may be set in the future, in a fantasy land or in the historical past—

but it is usually a single-title book. (There are some exceptions: Some literary fantasies are released in trilogies; and single-title original paperbacks are becoming more popular.) The characters are more fully developed, there are more subplots and a theme will run throughout the book. The depth of the story, the fullness of characterization, the richness of the language and the use of poetic devices set mainstream novels apart from series fiction. YA literature has a lasting quality; readers may remember the characters and stories all their lives.

Writing a young adult mainstream novel is every bit as challenging as writing an adult mainstream novel. The readers may be younger and less experienced in life, but they are no less intelligent. In school, these young adults are reading adult classics such as *The Red Badge of Courage*, *To Kill a Mockingbird*, *Huckleberry Finn*, *Of Mice and Men*, *Great Expectations*, *The Scarlet Letter*, *Brave New World*, *Crime and Punishment*, *Don Quixote* and *Lord of the Flies*. YA literature should be no less artistic. It should, however, be more relevant to young lives. Although teenagers have the capability to read adult literature, it is YA literature that they identify with because it is written *for* them and addresses their unique situation of being suspended between childhood and adulthood.

TOPICS FOR YOUNG ADULT LITERATURE

Because of TV, movies and news headlines, today's young readers are exposed to sex, violence and the darker side of human nature more than in recent generations. Remember the 1950s, when girls didn't date until they turned sweet sixteen? By contrast, today's girls are dating (and having babies) in junior high. News headlines depict teen parents murdering their newborn infants; drive-by shootings take lives of not only gang lords, but innocent bystanders; metal detectors often await students and visitors not only in high schools, but even junior highs in some areas of the country. How can fiction be any more disturbing than real life?

Contemporary mainstream novels often deal with realistic social issues—suicide, drugs, AIDS, sexuality, school violence, teen pregnancy, homelessness, runaways, war and racism. But expounding about the social issue is not the sole purpose of the novel. Such so-called "problem" novels are no longer popular.

Today's literary novels also incorporate universal themes such as coming of age, searching for one's identity or facing one's responsibility. The characters in these novels are on the brink of change, and by the end of the book they have grown and matured, often leaving the world of innocence and entering the world of reality. The endings do not need to be happy—indeed, they are often bittersweet—but they should contain an element of hope.

FEWER TABOOS

Literary YA novels have more freedom of expression than paperback fiction, which is aimed at the general masses. A mainstream author is able to take chances on controversial subjects and use language that is not acceptable in popular fiction. Recently, a few avant-garde YA novels have been published by editors willing to take risks with the censors. These books may include sex between unmarried teens, graphic profanity and homosexuality, all of which are considered taboo in mass market series fiction. Many such controversial books have won high critical acclaim: Francesca Lia Block's novella *Weetzie Bat* includes scenes of premarital sex with multiple partners, homosexual relationships and a planned teen pregnancy. But remember this paradox of writing YA literature: The more unique and controversial your story and characters, the more likely the book will be acclaimed. Yet, on the other hand, the more unique and controversial the story and characters, the more difficult it will be to find a publisher given the risk of censorship and resistance by schools.

Compared to series fiction, mainstream novels are difficult to write and sell. Rarely do they bring in big bucks. A typical YA hardcover novel earns an advance of about five thousand dollars and nothing more, but they are so rewarding to write. These are the books found on school library shelves, the books English teachers love to assign and the books that can influence and change young readers for the rest of their lives.

YOUNG ADULT POETRY

Another type of YA literature is poetry. The market for YA poetry is limited. Poetry to most teens is associated with the English classroom, and most of the poets are dead. Poetry can be written in rhyme or blank verse, with the latter preferable for adolescents. One exception is humorous poetry, which is even more outlandish when in rhyme.

Currently, the most likely market for selling a single poem is young adult magazines. (See Appendix for a list of selected titles.) To find out what editors are looking for in teen poetry, read as many young adult magazines as possible. Each magazine will have its own set of rules governing length, subject matter and style. You can also write to publishers for guidelines.

Finding a publisher for a YA poetry collection that you have penned yourself is challenging, but not impossible. Ideally, the poems will be connected by a common theme such as love, sports, school or other topics of interest to teenagers. For example, in Douglas Florian's collection of poems *Beast Feast*, the theme is animals. His collection *On the Wing* focuses on poems about birds. Another of his collections, *In the Swim*, centers on poetry about creatures in the ocean.

Some authors prefer to compile and edit anthologies of poems written by many different authors. Again, the poems should be tied together by a common thread. Lee Bennett Hopkins is a renowned master of such anthologies. Another award-winning anthologist of YA poetry is Paul B. Janeczko. Naomi Shahib Nye's collection of poetry, *The Tree Is Older Than You Are*, is a collection of poems written by Spanish-speaking poets. Most of the time, anthologists find the poetry in already published works, or they collect poetry written by children and teens. It is a difficult market, but, if poetry is your first love, do not give up.

PICTURE BOOKS FOR OLDER READERS

Within the past few years a new category of young adult literature has emerged—the picture book for older readers. Although fully illustrated and presented in the standard 32-page picture book format, these books touch on mature topics not normally addressed in picture books for children under ten years of age.

If you have not been in a high school, junior high or middle school recently, you may not realize how popular picture books have become as a teaching tool. Not only are they short and easily read in a few minutes, but like a poem, the subject matter is poignantly condensed into a few words. Today's highly visual teens appreciate the artwork. Though most teens would never buy a picture book for themselves, these books are good mechanisms for introducing curriculum-related topics.

Some recent picture book subjects include the race riots in Los Angeles, crack cocaine, gangland killings, death and war. One of the leading authors in this field is Eve Bunting. Her book *The Wall* is used to introduce students to the Vietnam War; her *Fly Away Home* leads into discussions of homelessness; and *Smoky Night* promotes the student discussions about race relations. All of these books have received high critical acclaim, and *Smoky Night* won the Caldecott Medal, the highest honor bestowed on a picture book.

These books are not always well-received by all reviewers, librarians and parents. Roger Sutton, editor-in-chief of *The Horn Book*, a review journal, stated in an on-line discussion, "I loathe those problem picture books," and his reviews of these books reflect his opinion. Some librarians fear that parents may become upset if young children mistakenly pick up these books thinking they are standard picture books. Most librarians agree that shelving YA picture books represents a problem, as these books do not fit neatly into either the picture book or young adult areas.

However, many education professionals see a need for such highly visual material, especially for teens who do not like to read longer books. My own *I Never Knew Your Name*, which addresses teen suicide, is used by high school and junior high social studies teachers. It was named an American Library Associaton (ALA) Recommended Book for Reluctant Young Adults and received the *Publishers Weekly* (PW) Cuffie Award for the Best Treatment of a Social Issue.

SHORT STORIES

Short does not mean easy. The short story is a literary style unto itself, having been mastered by such literary greats as Edgar Allan Poe, Nathaniel Hawthorne, Mark Twain, Katherine Anne Porter and Ernest Hemingway. Many of today's leading literary artists first published short stories in magazines or in collections. (For a list of YA magazines, see Appendix.)

Short stories are perfect for today's active teenagers who hardly seem to have time to sit still long enough to read a complete novel. A short story can be read in thirty minutes. They are clear and to the point, and the subject matter is as varied as that of novels. Common topics include romance, relationships, drugs, death, divorce, sports, college and careers. As in longer fiction, short stories can be written for entertainment or for more literary purposes.

Here are a few pointers to keep in mind when writing short stories for young adults.

1. The opening paragraphs should grab the reader's attention immediately. The beginning should tell the reader who the main character is, where the story is taking place, when it is taking place, and give an idea of what the conflict is all about.
2. Characterization must be developed quickly. The reader must be plunged into the protagonist's world immediately; first person is a useful device for achieving this. As in YA novels, the protagonist of the story should be slightly older than the age of the reading audience.
3. The number of characters and subplots in a short story must be limited. A typical short story has no more than three or four speaking characters.
4. The time span is shorter for short stories than for novels. Many short stories take place in a day's time or less, and rarely cover more than a week or two.
5. Every word must count. There is no room for flowery descriptions, long flashbacks or unnecessary dialogue. Strong verbs and nouns are critical to a short story.

To give you an example of an opening scene for a YA short story, I will use the one from my short story "Around the River Bend" which appeared in *Scholastic Scope* magazine. It begins:

> The helicopters would not let me sleep. At first I only heard a distant hum, no louder than the buzz of a hornet. Then, one by one, the silhouettes appeared over the top of the cedar-covered mountains. They moved across the face of the moon in formation like fat dragonflies with blinking red eyes. The hum turned into loud chop-chop-chops that echoed throughout the river canyon where we camped. The choppers performed maneuvers, following the leader like squatty black geese on a southward migration.

Chill-bumps rose on my neck at the sight of the machines. I knew that American soldiers from nearby Camp Wolters rode inside them, training for combat. The terrain in this part of Texas, steep hills thick with trees and shrubs, was similar to Vietnam. Vietnam—the very word nauseated me. How many of those men in the choppers would never come back? I wondered. How many of them would end up like my brother, Larry?

Many YA magazines are specifically aimed at either boys or girls, while others want stories that appeal to both, so it is important to read several issues of the magazine before submitting your manuscript. Word length for a typical YA short story ranges between 1,200 and 3,500, with the average story being closer to 1,800 words. Consult the magazine's editorial guidelines to determine an acceptable length. Most magazines pay short story authors by the word, with thirty-five cents per word being at the top of the scale.

For stories related to dated events (for example, the 500th anniversary of Christopher Columbus arriving in America or specific holidays), you must submit your article well in advance. There is usually at least a six month delay from the time your story is accepted until it is published. That means you will need to research, write and start submitting your story at least a year before the event.

Book-length short story collections are becoming more popular. Individual stories are tied together by a common theme. For two good examples of short story collections, read *Rio Grande Stories* by Carolyn Meyer and *Baseball in Spring* by Gary Soto.

Unlike collections, short story anthologies are books containing stories written by different authors. Again, a common theme connects the stories. Donald R. Gallo has edited several award-winning short story anthologies. His anthology *Ultimate Sports* is a collection of sports-related short stories written by outstanding YA authors. *Join in* contains multiethnic stories; *Short Circuits* focuses on shocking and unusual tales. *American Dragons*, edited by Laurence Yep, is a collection of stories written by Asian American students. An anthologist finds the stories for his collection by searching through published magazines, or sometimes will invite a well-known author to write a story specifically for the collection. The pay is usually a one-time flat fee.

LITERATURE IS TIMELESS

Because all topics are open game in YA literature, writers often try to choose their topic on the basis of trends. Without fail, at a writers conference someone asks a presenting editor, "What are some of the current trends?" or "What are you looking for?" And most editors respond, "We are looking for *good* books on any topic." Unless you are submitting to a weekly newspaper or magazine, most trends will have fizzled by the time you complete and mail your material. If you think back on your own adolescence, you will probably recall going through phases in your taste in clothing, music, foods and books. For me, grades five and six meant horse and animal books only. In junior high I became interested in the darker side, and Poe chilled my bones on many a sunny afternoon. Teenagers today are no different; their preferences in reading change. It is almost impossible to predict what the next trend will be; if it were possible, there would be a lot more millionaire YA authors.

Rather than worrying about what trend to write for or trying to guess which genre will sell the best, concentrate on what you like to write. After all, it is your time, hard work and money that will go into writing the book. There is nothing more torturous than writing something you do not care about; it becomes a homework assignment rather than a work of art.

Chapter Five

The Beauty of a Rainbow: Multicultural Young Adult Fiction

Adiscussion of today's young adult literature would not be complete without mention of multicultural writing, a growing category that reflects the changing demographics of American society. Where schools were once segregated and most children's literature was aimed at middle-class Caucasian readers, today's schools are more diversified. The school district where I live has students from over sixty nationalities. Schools not only have students from diversified backgrounds, but also teachers and administrators representing many ethnic groups. As today's textbooks account for cultural diversity, likewise today's YA literature has evolved to keep up with the needs of teachers and readers.

WHAT IS MULTICULTURAL LITERATURE?

The term *multicultural* is ambiguous, and there is still disagreement among experts regarding exactly what defines multicultural literature and who writes it. My 1990 Webster's dictionary does not contain the word *multicultural*, demonstrating that the term is a recent development. Although *culture* implies any group of people with similar traits, beliefs and customs, in reality, when Americans use the word *multicultural* they are usually referring to non-Caucasian cultures. Many publishers also place Jewish literature in the multicultural category, even though Judaism is a religion. The words *ethnic* and *minority* have also been applied to this literature.

For purposes of this book, when I use the term *multicultural* I am referring to writing about any culture of the world or any subculture within the United States. Whether writing a book about ancient Peruvians or modern-day Russians, the same challenges and research methods apply.

HISTORY OF MULTICULTURAL LITERATURE

Although the word *multicultural* has only become popular during the past ten to fifteen years, books about various cultures have been around a very long time. Rudyard Kipling wrote books about the children of India as early as the late 1800s; his novel *Kim*, published in 1901, is a classic. A look at the earliest Newbery Awards, which began in 1922, reveals many multicultural titles: *Tales from Silver Lands* (1925, South American Indians), *Shen of the Sea* (1926, Chinese), *Young Fu of the Upper Yangtze* (1933, Chinese), *Call It Courage* (1941, Polynesians), *Amos Fortune, Free Man* (1951, African slave), *Secret of the Andes* (1953, Peruvians), . . . *And Now Miguel* (1954, Mexicans), *Rifles for Watie* (1958, Cherokee) and *Island of the Blue Dolphins* (1961, Native Americans). With rare exception, these books were written by Caucasian authors who were not members of the cultures they described. This was the accepted trend until the 1960s when American publishers became more aware of cultural diversity.

In 1977, Mildred Taylor's book, *Roll of Thunder, Hear My Cry*, won the Newbery Medal and made history. Not only was it a book written about African-American children, it was also written by an African-American author. Authors from many diverse cultures entered the children's publishing field—Virginia Hamilton, Laurence Yep and Gary Soto, to name a few. The number of minority authors continued to increase through the 1990s. Today, some publishers devote entire catalogs to culturally diverse books.

As with any new category, multicultural books glutted the market for a time, and many were not written by authors of the culture depicted. In their haste to supply the demand for multicultural books, publishers often released books that contained cultural or historical inaccuracies or even stereotypes. I recall reading a highly acclaimed novel set in pre-Columbian times. Even though the book won many awards, it was full of errors about the food, clothing and culture of the indigenous people described.

Today, standards for multicultural fiction are much higher. Books will no longer be accepted just because they contain elements of another culture. The culture must be thoroughly researched and the people must be realistically portrayed and not stereotyped.

WHO WRITES MULTICULTURAL LITERATURE?

One of the most controversial issues in children's publishing today is the question of who should write multicultural books. One school of thought states that any author should be able to write about any culture as long as he or she does extensive research and portrays the culture accurately and honestly. Another school argues that only members of a specific culture have the understanding and ability necessary to write about that culture. Many publishers now insist that the author be a member of the culture depicted.

Having written several books about cultures other than my own, I agree with the first school of thought. In my opinion, some of the best multicultural literature today was written by nonmembers of the culture. Katherine Paterson (Japanese), Scott O'Dell (Native Americans), Linda Crew (Cambodians) and Gloria Whelan (Vietnamese) are just a few of the authors who have succeeded in this category. Yes, it is difficult to write about another culture—many times more difficult, perhaps, than writing about your own. Yet if you have a genuine interest in another culture and aren't just looking to fit the market, multicultural fiction can be immensely rewarding.

HOW TO WRITE ABOUT ANOTHER CULTURE

My most critically acclaimed books are those about the Vietnamese culture, so naturally people often ask me why I write about Vietnam. When I graduated from high school in 1966, I could not locate Vietnam on the map. I did not know a single thing about the country, except that the farmers wore baggy black pants and pointed hats, and that my friends and relatives were dying in muddy rice fields or steamy jungles. Back then, the word *Vietnam* evoked feelings of horror, anger and frustration in my heart.

Today, when I hear the word *Vietnam*, I think of beautiful misty mountains, sweet lotus flowers and peaceful villages where boys sit atop water buffaloes and play bamboo flutes. I think of a way of life that has existed for four thousand years, a culture that flourished long before Columbus peered at the New World through his spyglass. This transformation in my thinking came about through fifteen years of close friendships with Vietnamese families and years of intense research into the history and culture of Vietnam.

If, fifteen years ago, someone had asked me to write a book set in Vietnam, it would have been very different from *Song of the Buffalo Boy*, *Shadow of the Dragon*, *The Lotus Seed* or any of my forthcoming books set in Vietnam. Back then, I would have written such a book from the perspective of an American—how Americans were affected by the war and how they suffered. (There are many wonderful children's books written from such a perspective.) But today, that is not the kind of story I want to tell. I want to tell the stories from the point of view of the Vietnamese; I want to tell the story for my good friends who do not speak English well enough to tell the stories themselves.

The purpose of this chapter is to demonstrate how it is possible to write accurately and honestly about a culture or subculture outside your own. Before you begin, ask yourself these questions.

1. *Why do I want to write about this culture*? Did you pick a culture randomly because you think it is popular and will sell? Or do you have a close relationship with the culture? Maybe you are married to someone from the Southern Hemisphere, you lived in Saudi Arabia as a child, or you worked with Cambodians for many years. The greater your access to members of the culture you are describing, the easier it will be to become thoroughly acquainted with its customs.

2. *Can I tell my story with a protagonist that is not from that culture*? If you wrote your story with a Caucasian protagonist and then decided to change him or her to a minority person, you have not written a truly multicultural book. The culture must be an integral part of the character's personality, the plot and the setting.

3. *Would I want a member of the culture depicted to read my book*? If you are worried about the customs, religions, attitudes, clothing, food and so forth, to the point that you are reluctant to allow a member of that culture to read your book, chances

are you have not done enough research. You should have access to members of the culture who will be able to read and verify the facts in your book.

If you have answered all of the above questions honestly and feel that you have a story that must be told, a story you can tell only from the point of view of a protagonist from another culture, then you must be prepared to do abundant research. In essence, you have to submerge yourself in the culture until you no longer feel that you are a total stranger—until you are accepted as a friend. You must ask question after question about anything and everything, and be willing to listen to stories until your ears are ready to fall off. You must become an unobtrusive sponge, observing without causing distraction, because if you allow yourself to become the center of attention, those around you, especially the shy ones, will not act naturally. Once submerged in the culture, you will observe not only the differences between your cultures but also the similarities.

GET TO KNOW THE OUTER
TRAPPINGS OF THE CULTURE

To begin, you need to understand what makes the culture different from your own. The most obvious differences are the visible ones. This is what I call the *outer trappings* of a culture—food, clothing, music, festivals, holidays, language and occupations. I am fortunate to live in an area of the United States where there is a large Vietnamese population, with many Asian video, grocery and trading stores, shopping malls, restaurants, movie theaters, Buddhist temples and festivals. I am also fortunate to have many Vietnamese friends who never grow tired of answering my questions, even those questions that throw them into fits of laughter.

To get started, here are descriptions of the key outer trappings you should consider while researching the culture.

Setting. If your book takes place in another country, you will need to research the landscape and surroundings. The best way to do this would be to travel there, but that is not always possible. The next best thing is to interview people who have lived or recently traveled there. Ask them to show you their slides or home videos, and ask detailed questions. Finally, consult nonfiction books—travel guides, as well as photojournalism reference books about the country. Try to find books written by members of the culture or someone who lived in the country for many years; even novels can be helpful if written by someone from the culture. For *Song of the Buffalo Boy*, which is set in Vietnam, I interviewed Vietnamese Americans who had lived in the towns and villages I described. Rice farmers from the delta, fishermen from the coast, a doctor from Saigon, a teacher from Hue and a policeman from Da Nang—all were more than happy to tell me about their homes and towns in Vietnam. I also found two nonfiction books written by Vietnamese authors to be very helpful: *When Heaven & Earth Changed Places* has many scenes of rice villages, while *The Land I Lost: Adventures of a Boy in Vietnam* describes the lush environment of a small farming community in central Vietnam.

The setting should also evoke an atmospheric feeling that allows the reader to not only see the rain, but feel the heat, hear the birds and smell the food. Following is a list of setting characteristics you should thoroughly research:

- Terrain (flat, hilly, mountainous, sandy, rocky, fertile, desert, rivers, oceans)
- Weather (temperatures, seasonal changes, precipitation, wind, storms)
- Plants (trees, flowers, vegetation, planted crops)
- Animals (wildlife, domesticated livestock, working animals, pets)
- Transportation (horse, camel, oxcart, rickshaw, boat, train, car, taxi)
- Housing (tents, huts, straw, sod, adobe, brick, mansions)
- Populace (caravan, isolated farm, small town, village, rural, city)

If your story takes place in the United States, the setting must still reflect your chosen culture. For example, if your protagonist is Mexican, have his mother buy meat at the *carniceria* and bread at the *panaderia*, rather than at the local supermarket; his sister buy her records at the Spanish record shop; the words on shop doors and windows written in Spanish; and Spanish music drifting over the rooftops. In other words, do not place your protagonist in a typical, bland mall that could be found anywhere in America.

Foods. Another way to distinguish a culture is by its unique food. Start by eating at restaurants from the culture, if possible, but make sure that everything on the menu is authentic. Ask people from the culture to show you how to cook some traditional recipes. Buy cookbooks and shop at stores where members of the culture shop. Learn what foods are traditionally served for breakfast (in Vietnam, it's *pho*, a type of noodle soup), lunch and supper. Learn what time of day the different meals are served. What food, if any, is forbidden? Is beer or alcohol permitted? Do children drink the same beverages as adults? What types of dishes and utensils are used?

Respect the nuances of different cultures that come from similar regions of the world. For example, do not assume that all Southeast Asian food is alike. Vietnamese use *nuoc nam* (fish sauce), not soy sauce which is used more in China.

If your teenage protagonist is a member of an American subculture, he may eat hamburgers and pizza much of the time. In that case, you will need to include a special holiday or family occasion to provide a reason to include ethnic food.

Clothing. To learn about the clothing of inhabitants of a foreign land, study travel books with current photos, recent movies or slides taken by visitors, and, of course, ask members of the culture the names of specific items of clothing. Even those who wear Westernized clothing during the week may don ceremonial costumes for holidays and other special events. Or, as often is the case, the teenage protagonist may dress like any other American teen, but the parents or grandparents wear something more traditional.

Religion. Even if the culture's religion does not play an important role in your story, you will want to have a basic understanding of it. If possible, attend at least one religious ceremony and politely inquire about what you observe. Notice religious symbolism in homes and cars, on jewelry and so on. For my research, because the majority of Vietnamese are Buddhist, combined with Confucianism and Taoism, I visited several Buddhist temples and attended both family and public ceremonies. I learned that ancestor worship is very important, and that a relative's day of death is remembered and celebrated more than the birthday. Many of the Vietnamese who have come to America to get away from Communism are Catholics. They may not burn incense and have an intricate family altar like their Buddhist counterparts, but even Catholic Vietnamese commemorate the death day of a beloved parent.

Holidays and festivals. Reference books will list the major holidays of a culture, but there is no substitute for actually attending a festival. Most major cities with diverse populations have a variety of festivals throughout the year. For example, the major festival in Vietnam is Tet Nguyen, the Lunar New Year. To appreciate the importance of this festival, I attended New Year's parties and celebrations in Houston for many years—not just the public celebrations that began with the lion dance and thousands of exploding firecrackers, but also private functions that were reserved for Vietnamese and their occasional guests. Even though I did not understand the words of the ceremonies, and often was the only Caucasian in attendance, I absorbed the "feel" of the occasion by observing. While writing a Cambodian folktale, I attended a celebration of the Cambodian New Year (which occurs in April) and watched the magnificent dancers. Even though Cambodia and Vietnam are neighbors, their religion and festivals are entirely different.

Language. Buy a bilingual dictionary in the language that the culture speaks. Large bookstores usually have a wide selection. Use foreign words sparingly throughout the novel, and only where their meaning will be understood. For example, the meaning of *non-la* becomes obvious in this passage: "Uncle Long pushed the cone-shaped hat over Loi's unruly curls. 'If you want to survive, do not remove this *non-la.*'" Use foreign words only to create a feel for the language. With any foreign word or phrase, verify the spelling and usage.

Entertainment. Learn what types of music the culture has: Visit music shops and listen to recordings of traditional as well as modern music. Attend movies, even if you do not understand what is being said. What kinds of food are served at the theater? Chinese theater snack bars serve bags of dried cuttlefish, dried plums and sweetened lotus seeds. Indian cinemas serve *samosas* right next to the popcorn.

Many cultures have their own magazines and newspapers. Buy some (many are handed out free at restaurants and grocery stores) and ask someone to translate a few of the articles and even the advertisements. Visit a nightclub to discover what types of music and dancing are popular. I was surprised to learn that Vietnamese and Chinese nightclubs play ballroom music—rumba, cha-cha, tango and mambo—as well as more modern music for the younger patrons. And amazingly, even children were allowed in the clubs.

History. Even if your story is set in contemporary America, you need to have a rudimentary understanding of the culture's history. I had to read extensively to learn about Vietnam's history. Just knowing the names of legendary Vietnamese heroes impressed my Vietnamese friends and made them realize that I truly wanted to learn their culture. When it comes to history and politics, however, sometimes it is best to get the information from books. Friends may have their facts wrong or may have a political agenda.

EXPLORE THE INNER HEART OF THE CULTURE

By now, you should have a good understanding of what your characters will wear and eat, what music they will listen to, what type of house they will live in and what occupations their parents have. All these things are observable with the human eye. They are, in a way, superficial. By themselves, these outer trappings are not enough to make your protagonist authentic. The next step is to understand those things that are unseen and unspoken. This is the inner heart of a culture; it comes from having grown up in the culture and having experienced its history with its customs, beliefs and morals. If you have not grown up in the culture, your best bet is to become acquainted with someone who did.

Customs. Many customs do not have a reason; you just take them at face value. You may ask someone why do they do such and such, but you will not always get an answer. Most customs have evolved over thousands of years and the original meaning has long been lost. Many customs are closely tied to religion. Taboos can be difficult for most Americans to understand, but you must respect them. For example, in Vietnam, to pat a child or adult on the head would be considered rude and insulting (like patting a dog) rather than a display of affection, as it is in the United States.

Superstitions. Superstitions, like customs, often have un-known origins. Many Americans avoid walking under a ladder, but how many of us can explain why? The same holds for beliefs in other cultures. Some things are simply thought to bring good or bad luck. For example, in Vietnam, watching a wedding procession pass by is considered bad luck, while watching a funeral procession will bring good luck. When using superstitions to add color, remember that it is often the older generation that is most superstitious.

Attitudes and mores. Attitudes and mores are often associated with religion and must be handled with care. You must avoid imposing your moral values onto a society. What Americans disapprove of—girls marrying at the age of twelve or thirteen, for example—may be perfectly acceptable elsewhere. On the other hand, what Americans consider normal may be horrifying to members of another culture.

My knowledge of Vietnamese attitudes comes from living near and observing Vietnamese families I know. I learned that many Vietnamese families in America are in turmoil because of clashes between the older and younger generations. The older generation was raised to respect elders, obey rules, study hard and respect teachers. Being a goof-off or failing in school would bring dishonor to a family. Although many young Vietnamese Americans still adhere to this old belief, many more are lured by the abundant distractions faced by all American students— movies, games, after-school functions, television and playing with friends. This conflict between the old and new is the main theme running through *Shadow of the Dragon*, where many of the incidents are based on true stories. To get Vietnamese teens' point of view, I only had to turn to the children whom I had "adopted" and known for years. I saw the heartaches reflected in the faces of the parents and grandparents when their families broke apart because of these conflicts.

EMPHASIZE SIMILARITIES

After more than fifteen years, I know that I still do not under-stand everything about the Vietnamese culture. There are many things that puzzle me, just as there are things about Americans that still puzzle Vietnamese who have lived here for as long as twenty-five years. No matter how much I love the Vietnamese culture and people, the fact remains that I was not born and raised in Vietnam; I did not live there and have not experienced the same prejudices in America that they have. Therefore, when writing about Vietnam, I had to realize my limitations; I avoided those aspects of the culture that I did not understand and emphasized those that I did. I discovered that no matter what the culture, all people share certain human traits.

Emotions. No matter how a person dresses or what they eat, all humans feel emotions—love, hate, humiliation, guilt, pride, anger, sadness, joy and fear. To write about a poverty-stricken Amerasian girl who was ostracized from her village because of her mixed Vietnamese and American blood, all I had to do was draw upon my own experiences. As a girl, I was from one of the poorest families in town. I knew what it felt like to be laughed at, to be an outcast with no friends. I knew what it felt like to think "I am ugly"; to be gangly and taller than other girls. In my heart, I was no different than a Vietnamese girl in a similar situation.

Physical experiences. Have you ever cut your finger, stepped on a sharp rock, run until your side hurt, shivered from the cold, perspired from the heat, been hungry or thirsty, fainted at the sight of blood, shaken with fright or vomited at the sight of something being killed? So it goes around the world.

Sensory experiences. Smell, taste, touch, sight and sound are things that all humans understand, no matter what the culture. Let your heroine deeply inhale the perfume of her favorite flower; have the hero love the feel of a piece of ebony as he carves it; show a boy admiring a beautiful sunset; have a girl smile at the sound of her favorite song; and allow your characters to relish fresh, cool water when thirsty.

♦ ♦ ♦

Why describe all of these human experiences? Because your hero must be human first and a member of his culture second. The hero should not be so different that readers cannot identify with him. When you endow your character with common human traits, readers learn that although the customs, clothing and food may be different, beneath it all beats a human heart. And in the long run, perhaps that is the true purpose and beauty of multicultural literature—to show readers that we are more alike than different.

Chapter Six

Truth Is Beauty: Writing Nonfiction

Over the course of a lifetime, most people read more nonfiction than fiction. Nonfiction is the tool by which we learn about people, places and things, both seen and unseen. Nonfiction can be as dry as a math textbook or as fascinating as the story of the *Titanic*. Several children's nonfiction works have won the prestigious Newbery Medal, including the first recipient in 1922, *The Story of Mankind*. Today, nonfiction works by renowned authors, such as Russell Freedman, are as respected and sought after as award-winning fiction. And, indeed, the best nonfiction resembles fiction in terms of its descriptive language, sense of plot and effective use of tension.

Nonfiction covers a vast array of material, but for the purposes of this book, I will not include textbooks because they are mostly written in-house by educators and experts in the field. The focus of this chapter will be creative young adult nonfiction published by educational presses and major children's publishers. Because publishing nonfiction involves steps that don't apply to publishing fiction, I will address those steps here. (If you are interested in writing fiction exclusively, you may want to skip ahead to Part IV.)

Over the past ten to fifteen years, the market for nonfiction has grown by leaps and bounds, especially for the lower grade levels. If you are over forty, you probably think of nonfiction in terms of dull books with black and white photos, often with people wearing outdated clothes and hairstyles. Today, however, nonfiction books are vivid and entertaining, with color photographs, illustrations and a writing style aimed at grabbing and holding the attention of young readers. At times, today's nonfiction is more entertaining than fiction.

Nonfiction can be divided into three major groups: educational, recreational and biographical. The largest market for nonfiction is found within educational institutions. These books are curriculum-related and are used by students as supplementary study material in the classroom. Although many of these books are entertaining to read, their main purpose is to educate young adults about specific topics. Books about science, social studies, math, health, government and history fall into this category, and both male and female students make use of them.

Recreational nonfiction includes materials related to a teenager's personal life. Typical topics include hobbies, sports, beauty, music, movie stars and social activities such as dating and dancing. These books and magazine articles are most often aimed at a specific gender.

Biographies combine aspects of the educational and recreational categories, for although biographies are educational, the subject may be an individual associated with recreational reading—for example, a sports figure or a celebrity. Biographies also resemble novels to the extent that they include dialogue and action scenes. Biographies may be divided into two subcategories: fictionalized and standard. A fictionalized biography contains accurate facts about the subject, but includes fictionalized dialogue and scenes based on what the author imagines *may* have happened. A standard biography contains no fiction whatsoever. Any dialogue used is taken from eyewitness accounts, diaries or interviews, and no scenes are created that cannot be documented.

Writing nonfiction requires using the left side of the brain that calculates math, solves puzzles and organizes. If you enjoy research but struggle with plot and characterization, nonfiction may be the perfect medium for you. But before investing your time in research and writing the proposal, consider the following important preliminary steps.

SELECT YOUR TOPIC CAREFULLY

Let's assume you have a captivating idea that you think would make a great nonfiction book. (For more information on where ideas come from, refer to chapter eight.) Unlike fiction, where each author's unique approach and style will result in many different novels about the same subject, in the world of nonfiction fact is king and books about a given topic tend to be similar. These books will contain the same information and, once a certain number have been published, the need for a new book may no longer exist.

For this reason, it is important to conduct a basic market survey before you begin. One of the best places to start your search is the *Subject Guide to Children's Books in Print.* Since many older teens read adult material, you will also need to check the adult *Subject Guide to Books in Print.* Note the title, author, copyright date and age level of each book similar to the one you have in mind. Next, go to public and local school libraries to find as many of the books as possible. Ask the librarians which titles are and are not popular. Look for older, out-of-print books that may still be popular. Even if there are many books on your beloved subject, don't despair. If nothing new has been written in twenty years, most of the books will be outdated, and this can become one of your selling points. Some topics become outdated as early as ten years after publication. This is especially true of books about hobbies and fads. Can you imagine a book about Rubic's Cubes or Pac-Man being pertinent today?

To learn what is being published right now, request catalogs from publishers. These catalogs come out at least twice a year and list forthcoming books. Educational publishers often have extensive series about specific topics, such as cultures of the world, endangered animals, famous sports figures and famous musicians. If you would like to write for a series, it is imperative that you contact the publisher for guidelines. Series books have strict rules regarding page length, number of chapters and chapter content. Publishers' addresses can be found in *Writer's Market* and *Literary Market Place* (see Appendix). The Society of Children's Book Writers and Illustrators (SCBWI) also publishes a list of educational presses that specialize in nonfiction.

Visit bookstores that specialize in children's books. Peruse the YA nonfiction section. Ask a clerk which nonfiction books are the most popular and why. If you know any teenagers, ask them what kinds of nonfiction they and their friends read and why. Make sure these teenagers understand what nonfiction is, or they may only mention books they use for homework assignments, forgetting to include books about beauty, sports or hobbies.

Drop by the local school district's office and pick up a curriculum guide to determine which subjects are being taught and which books are being used in middle, junior high and high schools. If your topic is educational, but is not studied in schools, your proposal will be more difficult to sell. On the other hand, if your topic is pertinent and you find only a few related books in print, you may have a strong selling point. However, if you find a large number of books on a specific subject and several of them are recent, your book will need to be unique to convince an editor to buy it.

SELECT A SPECIFIC AGE GROUP

When writing nonfiction, the age of the targeted reading audience is very important. Age will determine not only the subject matter of the work, but also the writing style, length, number of photos and vocabulary level. An eleven-year-old reader has very different needs and comprehension abilities than a sixteen-year-old. That is why it is so important to note the age level of the books already published when conducting your market research. If there are a hundred books about butterflies for elementary school students, consider writing one specifically aimed at teenagers taking a freshman biology class.

Young adult nonfiction is roughly broken into two age groups: ages eleven through thirteen and ages fourteen through seventeen, or grades six through eight and nine through twelve. Younger adolescents may still have some of the reading habits of middle-grade readers (ages eight through twelve) who still enjoy and are interested in reading a wide variety of topics. They may still like series and may even collect books. Subject matter is abundant, varied and may be very specific. The subject of butterflies, for example, may include books about monarch butterflies, books about collecting butterflies or books about the world's largest butterflies.

Younger adolescents are still reading for pleasure and not just for class assignments. They want to learn about topics in detail, and more than just the facts; they want the inside scoop—the more interesting or unusual, the better. They enjoy an upbeat writing style and colorful, captivating photographs. And they want the information and photos to be current—no beehive hairdos or cars with fins. Some typical topics for this younger YA group are crafts and hobbies, sports, nature, pets, science, social studies (other cultures), puberty, history, the entertainment industry, biographies, health and beauty (acne, diets, exercise, hairstyles and make-up), social situations and ways to earn money.

The older YA readers, in grades nine through twelve, do not read as much as their younger classmates. Very often they only read adult books, making this a harder market to crack. But adult books rarely address the specific needs and issues of older teenagers. Such topics include teen pregnancy and single parenthood, sexually transmitted diseases, drug and alcohol abuse, careers, college preparation, motorcycles and automobiles, learning to drive, health and beauty tips, clothes, sports and hobbies. These books are read for personal reasons, and the subjects are often topics of discussion in teen or young adult magazines.

Educational or curriculum-related nonfiction covers a vast array of topics, from science to social studies to history. These books contain the same subject matter as adult books, but the writing style is more relaxed and upbeat. Photos often depict teenagers rather than adults.

Whatever category of YA nonfiction you choose, there is one thing all experts agree on: Do not try to write a nonfiction book appealing to all age groups. If you do, your book may end up appealing to no one.

CONSIDER PHOTOGRAPHS

Given the fact that today's adolescents have grown up in a world saturated with visual stimuli, such as TV, videos and movies, photographs are now more important to a work of nonfiction than in the past. Lively, attractive color photos and detailed illustrations are expected. If students associate nonfiction with the drudgery of schoolwork, vivid photographs may help to convince them otherwise.

Many publishers require authors to provide their own photos. Before submitting your proposal, determine if you have a source for photographs. You may be skilled enough to take them yourself, but remember that publishers demand very high quality and a wide variety of material. If you do not feel you are able to take good photos, or if the subject matter is one for which you have limited access, you will need to obtain photographs elsewhere.

One economical way to find photographs is through government agencies—city, state or federal. For photographs of particular cities or towns, contact the appropriate tourism department or the Chamber of Commerce. The U.S. government is also a bountiful source for many topics. For example, if your book is about hurricanes, contact the U.S. Department of Commerce, specifically the National Oceanographic and Atmospheric Agency. Write to NASA if you are writing about space, rockets or shuttles. For my nonfiction book about Vietnam, I purchased several war photos from the U.S. Army, Air Force and Navy. The Library of Congress and National Archives have millions of photographs, and a visit to Washington, D.C. can uncover vast numbers of photographs.

To obtain addresses and phone numbers of the hundreds of U.S. government agencies, check out *Information U.S.A.* by Matthew Lesko (Penguin Books). Other useful references for government resources are *Special Collections in the Library of Congress: A Selective Guide*, compiled by Annette Melville; *Archives: A Guide to the National Archives Field Branches*, by L.D. Szucs and S.H. Luebking; and *The United States Government Manual*, published by the National Archives and Records Administration. The average price for a copy of a government-provided photo is about thirty-five dollars.

Local libraries are reliable research sources. For historical material, consider historical societies or universities. Many university archives contain documents, paintings, artifacts and photographs. Universities are also a good source for more up-to-date material, from photos of telescopes from an astronomy department to diagrams of cell structure from the biology department. Private research institutions and hospitals often furnish science- and health-related photos. And museums are wonderful sources for a variety of materials from dinosaur bones to semiprecious gems to Indian artifacts.

Another approach to acquiring photos is to study books already published on the topic. Look up the photo credits, usually listed in the front or back, and write to the source asking if they have any additional photos. If you see something promising in a periodical, write to the news service that provided the photo or to the periodical's art department. In your letter, mention the date and title of the article and the page where the photo appeared.

Local newspapers may also prove fruitful and the photos may be easier to access. When I saw a photo of Vietnam in a local newspaper, I contacted the person who had taken it, a local university history professor. As it turned out, he had just returned from Vietnam and had hundreds of beautiful color slides. He allowed me to use all of them free of charge in exchange for photo credits and a few complimentary copies of the book.

A more expensive source for photographs is from news agencies, such as the Associated Press, United Press or Reuters. These organizations have large stocks of historical material from the past seventy-five years, but be warned: Such photos may cost one hundred dollars or more each.

Lastly, you may have to resort to stock photo companies. These are companies that buy photos from professional photographers from around the world and then sell the right to use the photos to authors, advertising agencies or anyone in need of a good photo. The quality is excellent and the subject matter is broad, but the price is very high—up to several hundred dollars for use of a single color photograph. (See Appendix for a list of photo sources.)

No matter what the source, you must obtain permission for any photo you use, even one taken by your own mother or spouse, to avoid copyright infringement. The publisher will insist you have signed permission forms. The exception is government agencies because those photographs are considered in the public domain (but you will still need to list them in the photo credits). When contacting the photo source, ask for one-time nonexclusive world rights. This means you have the right to use the photo only in the specific book you describe in the permission letter. It also means that you do not have exclusive rights; i.e., another author may also use the same photo in his book at the same time you do. If you decide to write another book on a similar topic, even for the same publisher, and want to use the photo again, you must obtain permission once more and will probably have to pay anew for the use of the photo.

When selecting photographs, keep the age of the readers in mind. The readers will appreciate seeing someone their own age or slightly older. Also, the subject matter and tone of the photos should match the subject matter and tone of the text. If your topic is bouncy and humorous, you would not want photos of death and famine.

The publisher will usually tell you approximately how many photos will be needed. Sometimes this will be as little as one per every two pages, or as many as two per page. Try to provide more than the required amount. For example, if you need a single shot of an elephant, send two or three different photos so that the editor has some leeway in terms of contrast and other technical considerations. Don't be surprised if the editor rejects many of your photos and asks you to provide others. The quality must be excellent in order for a photograph to be reproduced in a book.

Most publishers will tell you in what format the photos must be. Typically, a black-and-white photo will be a glossy 8×10, while the preferred format for color photos is slides. Be sure you know what will be expected before purchasing the photos, or you may waste a lot of money. And be certain you understand as to whether you will be responsible for purchasing the photographs. There are exceptions, but many educational publishers require the author to pay for all the photos. This should be in your contract. Read it very carefully to avoid unexpected expenses.

RESEARCH IS NECESSARY

After you have selected a topic and an age level, you will need to do some preliminary research to write an intelligent and interesting query letter, outline and proposal. (After you have sold the project, you may conduct more in-depth research).

Because research is so important to writing both nonfiction and fiction, chapter nine is devoted to that subject. For now, just remember that if you do not enjoy research, it is very unlikely that you will be happy or successful as a nonfiction author. Although some fiction can be created without in-depth research, it is impossible to write nonfiction without hours spent researching at the library, on location and conducting interviews.

THE NONFICTION QUERY LETTER

For nonfiction projects, it is standard procedure to have a contract in hand before writing the book. (The exception would be a very short work, such as a nonfiction picture book or a magazine article.) To spend years on research and writing without a contract is comparable to quitting your job and putting the family's savings on a roulette table in Las Vegas. You may win, but most likely you will have spent your money and effort in vain. So, after you have found a good topic, done your market study and completed your preliminary research, your next step is to sell the proposal to the editor. This process begins with a first-rate query letter.

A *query letter* is a brief one-page letter in which the author asks the editor for permission to send either a proposal or a completed manuscript. I have heard authors lament that it is easier to write an entire book than it is to write a query letter. Some authors do not bother with a query letter at all, but send a proposal to the editor cold and unsolicited. There are many good reasons to query. First, it is polite. The letter serves as an introduction. Second, if the editor does request you to send a proposal, the proposal then becomes solicited and is more likely to succeed.

Query letters save you the time, effort and expense of sending out lengthy proposals that may be rejected. The editor's response to your letter may provide you with market information or suggestions, and the response to a query is usually much faster than the response to a proposal or manuscript. If you wish to write for a nonfiction series, it is crucial to query first, as the publisher may have a book on your topic already contracted. Many writers market publications will tell you if the publisher requires a query first. Some publishers require queries for longer works, but prefer the entire manuscript for shorter ones. A nonfiction picture book or a nonfiction magazine article should be sent in its entirety with a cover letter.

The query letter, in many ways, is like a job interview or a sales pitch. In one page you must convince an editor to request your proposal or manuscript. This means using good quality paper, 1″ to 1½″ margins and clear, readable print. Unlike a manuscript, the query letter is single-spaced, should be no longer than one page and should contain the following information.

Paragraph One—Introduction. Immediately let the editor know that your proposed project is a nonfiction book for young adults. Mention if it is aimed specifically toward girls or boys and the estimated word length. If it is to be one of the publisher's series books, also mention that. (If it is to be a series book, you should have sent for the series guidelines and studied them beforehand.) This is a good place to let the editor know that you are familiar with the publisher's books, and that you feel your book will fit into their nonfiction list. If you have met the editor, let her know. If you have recently read an article she wrote, or a market report in which she stated that she was looking for a certain kind of book, also mention that in your first paragraph.

Paragraph Two—Brief description of your proposed book. Briefly summarize the book and its purpose. Write clearly and concisely in the same style that the book will be written. Convey your enthusiasm while making the topic sound interesting.

Paragraph Three—The market for the book. Explain why your book is needed and why you believe it will sell. Mention that you have researched the market and found few books for this age level, that the ones you found were outdated, or that your approach will be unique from all the other books. If the topic is studied in school curriculums, say so here. Mention that librarians feel there is a great need for more literature on this topic. Perhaps you can mention that the students you spoke with are excited and curious about the topic. If the book is tied to an upcoming event, let the editor know. (If you prefer, paragraphs two and three may be combined into one, as long as the necessary information is covered.)

Paragraph Four—Your writing or professional credentials. Although nonfiction publishers will accept books by unpublished writers, it is advantageous to mention any of your published works, even if they are not in the children's market. Also, explain what qualifies you to write the book. For nonfiction, your profession and background are often as important as your writing credentials. Perhaps you are a university history professor, your hobby for the past twenty years has been beekeeping or you lived in Borneo for ten years.

Now is also the time to mention how you will obtain photographs.

Paragraph Five—Closing. Thank the editor for her time and ask if she would like to read the proposal, which will include sample chapters. If the manuscript is already complete, be sure to let the editor know this. She may want to skip the proposal altogether. Tell her you are looking forward to hearing from her in the near future and that you have included either a self-addressed stamped envelope (SASE) or a self-addressed stamped postcard for her convenience.

It is common courtesy to include a SASE for the editor's reply. However, I have found that a self-addressed stamped postcard receives a much faster response. The editor only has to sign her name and date and then drop it in the mail.

Keep records of where and when you mailed the queries, and be patient. Response time for queries is faster than responses for proposals or manuscripts, but you may still have to wait several weeks.

NONFICTION PROPOSAL

Whether your query received a positive response or you decide to send an unsolicited proposal, your proposal will contain the same elements: a cover letter, title page, table of contents, introduction (overview), author bio/resume, outline of book, sample chapter(s), reply card, SASE and supplemental material (sample photos, published writing samples, sample bibliography and so forth).

The cover letter for a *solicited* proposal or manuscript should be very brief, thanking the editor for requesting the material. If the proposal or manuscript is being submitted to other publishers, mention that here, but it is not necessary to divulge the number or names of the other publishers. A simple statement such as "Another publisher has also requested this proposal" will suffice. Always verify that a publisher will accept multiple submissions before sending it. Since your earlier query contained a lot of information, there is no need to repeat it in the cover letter.

If, however, the letter is accompanying an *unsolicited* proposal or manuscript, it should follow the same format as the one-page query letter, with four or five paragraphs. In this case, begin by saying something like "Enclosed for your consideration, please find the proposal for a nonfiction young adult book entitled *Borneo! . . .*" , as opposed to "May I send you the proposal for a nonfiction YA book entitled *Borneo!*?"

The title page will include your name, address and phone number in the upper left-hand corner. Approximate word length appears in the upper right-hand corner. Drop down and center the title (in all caps) and byline (standard type) in the middle of the page.

Each subsequent page should have a header (also called a *slug*) with key words from the title and your last name in the upper left-hand corner. For example, the header for a book proposal for *Borneo! Land of Surprises*, submitted by a Mr. John Smythe, would look like this:

Proposal—Borneo!/Smythe   5

Some authors prefer their name on the right-hand side of the header, next to the page number, rather than on the left-hand side. For example:

Proposal—Borneo!   Smythe—5

The table of contents will list everything included in the proposal and the page numbers. (This is not the table of contents for the book itself, which will be referred to here as the *outline*.)

The introduction will include much of the same information as in the query letter, only in greater detail. Running one or two pages in length, it will contain information about the topic, who will read the book and why, whether there are other books like it, how it relates to school curriculums or popular teen hobbies, and so forth. Mention resources available to you for your research and photos, as well as any interviews you will conduct and any personal or occupational experience related to the topic. If you have connections or know specific ways to promote the book, be sure to include this information. If you do volunteer work with teens or are associated with them in any way, this can also be helpful because it shows that you are in touch with their world. And don't forget to expound on the back matter, the pertinent information, such as appendices, glossary, bibliography and lists of organizations and agencies, at the end of the book. Include the proposed length of the finished manuscript and the expected completion date. Some authors refer to the introduction as an *overview*.

The author bio, sometimes called a *vita*, is different from the standard resume you give to a prospective employer at a job interview. The bio is one page in length, double-spaced and written in the third person with complete, engaging and interesting sentences. Open the bio with a hook, and only include information that is pertinent to your ability to write the proposed book. For example, if you are writing about Borneo, the fact that you worked part time as an auto mechanic for five years is not pertinent. Describe your writing credentials (if you are very widely published, you may need to attach a separate page). If you have published only periodical articles, you can summarize; for example: "Mr. Smythe has written over one hundred articles for young adult magazines such as *Young Miss, Boys Life* and *National Geographic, Jr.*" Stress the published works that are related to the topic of your proposed book. If you have not published at all, do not bring this fact to the attention of the editor. Also, mention any organizations that you belong to, if they are related to writing or to the topic.

Here is a bio for our fictitious author who wants to write a book about Borneo.

> John Smythe fell in love with Borneo at the age of seven while living there with his missionary parents. While his friends back home in Indiana played football and learned to dance the twist, John tracked lizards in ancient forests and learned to use poison blow darts from indigenous tribesmen.
>
> After ten years in Borneo, John returned to the United States and received his Ph.D. in Southeast Asian cultures at Harvard. Following a thirty-year teaching career at the high school and college levels, Mr. Smythe now devotes his time to writing, travel and photography. Of the many articles he has published in educational journals and adult and young adult magazines, twenty-three focus on the people, places and wildlife of Borneo. Smythe is president of the Friends of Indonesia Association, and often visits his missionary brother who still lives in Brunei. Smythe's pho-

tographs have won international awards and have appeared in periodicals around the world.

Smythe hopes that this book will encourage American teens to see the beauty and uniqueness of Borneo's fascinating and ancient culture.

The outline of the proposed book is the heart of the proposal and will take much time and effort to prepare. The editor will be looking at the outline to determine how you organize material and handle transitions between subjects.

There are three types of outlines. One is the traditional *word outline* you learned in English class—Roman numerals followed by capital letters, followed by Arabic numbers, followed by lower case letters. This type of outline conveys the organization and contents of the book, but tends to be dry and does not show the editor your writing style.

To provide a better sense of how you write, you may opt for the *sentence outline*, which follows the same format as the word outline but uses brief sentences to describe each category and subcategory.

The most revealing type of outline is the *chapter-by-chapter outline*, which briefly summarizes the chapters, usually devoting approximately one page to each chapter. This type of outline allows the editor to not only see how the book will be organized, but also provides a longer sample of your writing style.

In each of the outlines, describe the back matter contents. And remember, no matter which outline you use, it will be your most valuable tool when writing the text; you will refer back to it again and again.

Sample chapters are an important part of your proposal because they demonstrate your writing style. You should include at least chapter one and another chapter or two from later in the book. (Chapter one typically has a lot of general introductory material and often does not demonstrate the true character of the overall book). Your sample chapters should be as polished and captivating as possible. Select chapters that show your enthusiasm, the uniqueness of your research and the most interesting aspects of your manuscript. If you have original material that has never appeared in published works, use that as your sample chapter. For example, our illustrious John Smythe would include a sample chapter that describes some of his own adolescent experiences in Borneo and photos he took while there.

Optional material may be added at the end. This would include tear sheets or photocopies of published articles, copies of one or two interesting photographs, a sample chart or illustration if you are an artist (but never send your original artwork), a few sample glossary terms and some of the research resources you have or will use.

Always include a SASE with enough postage for the return of your proposal. Also enclose a self-addressed stamped postcard for the editor to let you know that he or she has received the proposal. The postcard contains the following information: name of the manuscript, a line for the editor's signature, a line for the date received and three blank lines for the editor to make comments, if so desired. (See Appendix for sample acknowledgment card.) Very often editors will write in the estimated time it will take to consider the proposal. Don't be amazed if you wait several months for a response—children's publishers are always flooded with submissions—but the more professional your proposal, the more likely you will receive a fast response.

MAKING NONFICTION APPEALING TO TEENS

Once you have received that exciting phone call or letter from the editor making you an offer for your nonfiction project, you will carry out more in-depth research, gather photographs and begin the process of writing the text. When writing nonfiction for children and young adults, it is important that you maintain an upbeat style. Stuffy, pedantic writing will only make the reader put the book down.

Your writing must be clear, accurate and unbiased. Because the main market for nonfiction includes schools and public libraries, your work must first pass the test of educators and librarians. If you are obviously biased and have manipulated the facts to fit a personal agenda, schools will be less likely to purchase your book. Whether we agree or not, objectivity is very important to publishers who are trying to please as wide a market as possible.

Whatever the purpose of your book—educational, biographical or recreational—it should have a beginning, middle and end, with a unifying theme tying all the chapters together. The length of the chapters will vary, but generally nonfiction today is shorter than in the past. Allowing for photographs, which often can take up to half a page, a typical chapter will have approximately ten manuscript pages. If you are writing for a series, the guidelines clarify exactly how many pages the chapters should be. Each chapter title should give an indication of the chapter's contents, yet be interesting in itself.

A good nonfiction book begins each chapter with a "grabber." Here is an example of a great hook from a nonfiction book, *San Antonio* by Sally Lee. The chapter about festivals and celebrations is entitled "Viva Fiesta!" and opens like this:

> A boy smashes an eggshell over his friend's head and laughs as confetti spills out. *"Viva Fiesta!"* he yells as he runs off to find his next victim. His friend isn't mad. Being hit with a *cascarone*, or confetti-filled eggshell, is part of the fun of Fiesta San Antonio.

Pacing implies the fluctuation between fast- and slower-paced material. Do not weigh down a paragraph or a page with too many facts; mix in a quote, anecdote, personal experience, song, poem or photograph.

Each chapter ends with a brief summation of the chapter and enticingly leads into the next one. Here is the ending paragraph for Lee's chapter about festivals:

> San Antonio is a fun-loving city that even celebrates some unpleasant things. Each January, when the river is drained so that the banks and riverbed can be cleaned and repaired, a Mud Festival is held. There are a Mud King and Queen, mud sculpture contests and all sorts of dirty delights! It shows how far some people in San Antonio will go to find a reason to enjoy themselves.

This closing nicely sums up the chapter's theme on festivals and flows into the next chapter, entitled "Just for Fun," which is about recreational activities. In a well-written nonfiction book, the conclusion ties in with the opening, giving the reader a feeling of having gone full circle. In *San Antonio,* the last paragraph summarizes the preceding chapters, creating a sense of fulfillment and completion.

> San Antonio is a mixture of many different things. It is one of the oldest cities in Texas, yet it is full of modern

buildings and industries. Its military bases make it important to the United States, yet its traditions give it a strong link to Mexico. Its people value the city's past, yet they work hard to improve its future. All these things make San Antonio a pleasant city to live in, work in, and visit. It truly is a magical city.

The last sentence refers back to the book's very first sentence: "There is magic in downtown San Antonio."

Nonfiction is becoming increasingly popular and is often an easier market to break into for the unpublished writer. But before you begin researching and writing, whether for fiction or nonfiction, there are several steps you should take to prepare yourself.

PART THREE

First Things First: Four Steps for Getting Started

Chapter Seven

Step One:
Think Like a Writer

Say the words *writer* and *author* and what images come to mind? A hard-drinking, hard-living, suicidal malcontent? A headstrong prima donna who orders her secretaries about like dogs? A shy, secluded hermit working by lantern light in the deep woods, so oblivious to the world that his beard has icicles hanging from it? A sleuth who solves all the murders that just happen to occur in every town she visits? A brilliant but weird intellectual who lives in an ivory tower? A rich and famous person living in a mansion on a cliff overlooking the sea?

All the above personas have been depicted in the fiction of movies, TV, novels and the media. The image of the rich and famous author is probably the most intriguing; unfortunately, it's also the least realistic. You may occasionally hear about an author receiving a million dollar advance, or selling millions of copies of his best-seller, but those people are newsworthy because they are the *exceptions* to the rule, not the norm. You rarely hear about the thousands of average writers. In fact, less than 1 percent of all writers are able to support themselves solely by writing. In reality, most authors either barely eke out a living solely by writing, have a second job, or generate additional income through lectures.

Of course, there are many successful authors in every category, including young adult, but even successful authors are likely to lead mundane lives more akin to successful business entrepreneurs. An author usually has an office, business equipment, specific goals, schedules and deadlines, expense ledgers, tax ID numbers, rows of reference books, subscriptions to professional publishing and review periodicals and several library cards.

In a nutshell, here are several things you can do to help yourself establish good writing habits and think like a writer.

ESTABLISH WRITING GOALS

Every project, no matter how complicated or seemingly difficult, from baking a cherry pie to building a pyramid, can be achieved if goals are set and reached one step at a time. Although the thought of writing a young adult novel and selling it to a publisher, or negotiating a contract with an editor, may send shivers of trepidation down your spine, the thought of taking an evening off to read a YA novel or typing a single page a day shouldn't sound so difficult.

Following is a list of goals I have used for years. It can apply to any project, no matter how large or small.

1. Establish annual goals. Every January 1, write down at least three major goals you want to accomplish that year, such as:

   a. Complete a YA novel and submit it to a publisher.
   b. Save money to buy a computer and printer.
   c. Take a college course in creative writing.

Be realistic. If you list fantasy goals like "become rich and famous" or "win the lottery" you are setting yourself up for failure.

2. Establish monthly goals. Under each of the three major goals write a goal for each month. For goal *a*, you could list the following:

   January—write synopsis and rough outline for YA novel
   February—do major research
   March—write rough draft for chapters 1–5
   April—write rough draft for chapters 6–10
   May—write rough draft for chapters 11–15
   June—write final draft for chapters 1–5
   July—write final draft for chapters 6–10
   August—write final draft for chapters 11–15
   September—polish and edit manuscript
   October—work on query letter, synopsis and outline

November—study markets; mail query to appropriate
    publishers
December—mail proposal or completed manuscript

3. Establish weekly goals. Break your monthly goals down
even further into weekly goals. You will need to get the calendar
out. Use actual dates; for example:

Jan. 1 through Jan. 5—work on synopsis
Jan. 8 through Jan. 12—work on plot
Jan. 15 through Jan. 19—work on character development
Jan. 22 through Jan. 27—work on outline

In March, when you are writing the rough draft, a goal may be:
March 1 through March 5—write rough draft for chapter one.

4. Establish daily goals. Daily goals are what some people
call *To Do* lists. The schedule varies, depending on your personal lifestyle. If you work full time, you may only be able to
write on weekends, late at night or early in the morning. It may
be impossible for you to write every single day due to family
commitments, but it is important to get into the habit of writing
as much as possible. If your daily goals are realistic, such as
"write one page a day" or "complete one scene a day," you will
steadily progress toward your ultimate goal.

I remember well writing my nonfiction book *Vietnam: Re-
building a Nation.* I worked full time from 7:00 A.M. until 3:30
P.M. As soon as I got home, around 4:00 P.M., I took a nap, then
worked on my book until midnight or 1:00 A.M. I then woke up
at 5:30 A.M. in order to get to work before 7:00 A.M. I slept during
my thirty-minute lunch break. It was rough—some nights I
wrote only one page—but the manuscript progressed and was
turned in on time.

5. Allow yourself some goof-off time. Setting goals that
are too tough or unrealistic can lead to burnout and feelings of
frustration and failure. I always add a few goof-off days in my
schedules, much like schools add snow days to theirs. You also
should figure in days off to attend conferences and to visit research sites, as well as for family reunions, holidays and so forth.

6. Review your progress. Only you know your abilities, limitations and desires. I try to write one YA novel a year; I have a
friend who is happy to write one every three years; another

writes one every two months. If you find that you are not reaching any of your goals or are not writing at all, you may have writer's block, a fear of failure or success. Chapter nineteen discusses some of these ever-present aspects of the writing life. Your goals are a very personal thing but, no matter what they are, each time you achieve one it will give you a tremendous feeling of satisfaction and accomplishment.

SET UP A WRITING AREA

Every author needs a place to work. It doesn't have to be fancy or elaborate. I wrote my first two adult novels at my kitchen table—a table covered with papers, research books and note cards. I wrote my first YA books while living in an apartment where the only place for the typewriter was on a tiny desk in the bedroom. Don't worry about windows, carpets or wall coverings: Those things don't matter. What does matter is that everyone in your household knows that while you are in your writing space you are not to be disturbed. If you have small children, you may have to wait until they are asleep to write; if you have older children, you may have to wait until they are at school.

I'm the first to admit that working mothers have it harder than any other group of writers. I know an author who spends his days merrily writing his novels, and then hands the manuscripts to his wife to proofread and edit. Few writers have it that easy, but many of today's most successful female authors manage to balance writing with working outside the home, children, husbands and pets. One famous YA author tells the story of how she and a neighbor took turns babysitting for each other's children. On her day off, she would write like crazy with no disturbances.

INVEST IN DEPENDABLE EQUIPMENT

I know a very successful author who writes the first draft of her wordy historical romances longhand while swinging in a hammock. Another famous author uses an old manual clunker (about a 1940 vintage) for his first drafts. Both authors claim that their methods force them to slow down and think more clearly.

In other words, for your rough draft, the equipment isn't critical. The main purpose is to get the words on paper. But when it comes to the final draft, nothing beats a computer for editing and revising, shifting paragraphs and inserting left-out words.

The two major types of personal computers (PCs) are Macintosh and IBM-compatible. Macintosh has a reputation for high quality, but IBM-compatible PCs are more abundant and usually less expensive. New IBM-compatible PCs come equipped with Windows operating system. If you buy an older PC, avoid one which only has DOS, since most people find Windows more user-friendly. Whatever brand you choose, you will need word processing software. The two most common word processing programs are WordPerfect and Microsoft Word. Both of these programs are available for Macintosh, DOS or Windows.

Besides a computer, you will also need a good printer. These range in quality and price. Avoid the old dot matrix printer as many publishers refuse to accept manuscripts printed on them. Next in quality comes the ink-jet printer. These continue to improve, but they do present the occasional danger of ink-smear. The best printers, in my experience, are laser printers. They cost a bit more, but create a professional appearance.

Finally, if you intend to make use of the many resources available through the Internet, you will need a modem. If your computer does not have an internal modem, you may purchase one as a peripheral. (The benefits of the Internet are discussed in following chapters.)

Some writers purchase the cheapest, and often most inefficient, equipment and end up with manuscripts that don't look their best. If you cannot afford top-of-the-line equipment, look in the classified ads. You can often find a used computer and printer that are only a few years old, slightly outdated but still in excellent condition, that will suit your purposes.

A final thought on equipment: It is only as capable as the person using it. A middle-school student once asked me if I had some tips on how he could prepare himself to become an author—which courses to take in college and so forth. My instant reply was take a typing class. It sounds trivial, but it is one of the basic facts of today's world: You cannot submit handwritten manuscripts to publishers. The more you understand office equipment, the fewer headaches you will have. If you are a poor typist or don't know much about computers, by all means take a class. It will save you hours of frustration in the long run.

CULTIVATE SELF-DISCIPLINE AND MOTIVATION

Whether we like it or not, being a writer requires self-discipline. Without it, writing projects do not get done. I often hear authors say that they love to write, they cannot live without it, they can't wait to get up in the morning to write that next chapter, their day flies by and they don't even stop to eat lunch. Whew! How I wish that were the case for me. Unfortunately, getting my bottom in place and my fingers typing is like dragging the cat to a flea dip. But on the other hand, the knowledge that if I don't write, I don't get paid, and if I don't get paid, I don't eat, gets me motivated.

If you are not published and your income does not depend on selling that next article or novel, you must reach deep inside yourself for motivation and discipline. One way to do this is to imagine yourself as a successful author. Imagine that you are independent and self-sufficient, your writing receives rave reviews, you have a nice income and some fame. You speak at schools and conferences, and neighborhood kids ask for your autograph. Think of all the fan letters you will receive from adoring adolescents, and of all the lives you will influence with your words. Think about the good aspects of being a writer every day before you start writing. Picture yourself being successful.

Another approach to motivation is the self-reward system. After accomplishing your daily or weekly goal, reward yourself with something you want or enjoy. (It's important to deny yourself that item until you've met your goal.) Sometimes its as small as eating a chocolate-covered peanut when you finish the end of the page, doing a little gardening at the end of the day or renting a movie at the end of the week. But most important is the reward that comes from knowing that you have set a goal, stuck to it and completed a project.

KEEP IN TOUCH WITH THE YOUNG
ADULT PUBLISHING INDUSTRY

All right! You're on your way to thinking like a writer. You've set writing goals, established a writing space and have disciplined and motivated yourself to write often.

There's an old saying that writing is a lonely profession. True, you do not have co-workers hovering around your desk and you don't go to the nearby restaurant with them for lunch, but an author does not live in a vacuum. Authors are professionals and as such must do the same things as other professionals. Doctors are expected to keep abreast of current medical news and equipment, attend conferences, talk to experts in the field and so forth. It is no different for writers. Whether you are published or not, here are some ways to keep in touch with the young adult publishing industry.

Read Young Adult Literature

It never ceases to amaze me how many people I meet say they want to write YA books but haven't read any since they were adolescents. Read, read, read. Start with the Newbery winners and the books that get the starred reviews (the stars beside a review signify excellence), but don't stop there. Read YA paperback series—mysteries, horrors and romances. Discover what characterizes each genre. This will help you find your niche. Read hardcover and paperback books. Read old classics and new best-sellers. Read books by the great YA authors of today and yesterday, and read the ones you've never heard of. If you find something you think is terrible, use it as an example of what not to do. If you read something inspiring or moving, use it as an example of what to strive for. Read to determine what kinds of books are being written, what subjects are being written about and how old the protagonists are. Read to learn how good authors handle dialogue, plot, pacing and characterization.

Talk to librarians at local middle and junior high schools and find out what the students are reading, both in English class and on their own. Ask the local school district for a copy of its curriculum. Most state library associations issue recommended reading lists that are available from school librarians. Read all the books on the list. You may be surprised by what's out there. I know I was. I did not start writing for young adults until 1991. Having graduated from high school in 1966, I missed out on the great YA revolution of the 1960s and 1970s. Catching up on two decades' worth of novels took a while, but it was worth it. I was shocked, amazed and thrilled. I knew I had found my niche.

Take a Writing Course

A writing course should not be considered an omniscient fountain of knowledge. Some writers never take writing classes and do just fine; others find these classes as a stimulating way to jump-start creative juices. However, not all writing courses are created equally. If you live in a large city, there are probably writing courses offered by local colleges. Sometimes a famous author will offer classes or seminars. Talk to others who have taken the classes and weigh their results against the cost. The Highlights for Children Writers Conference at Chatauqua, New York, is one of the most famous conferences. Another is a correspondence course offered by the Institute of Children's Writers. Whatever you do, remember that there comes a point when you will already know what the teachers are teaching. At that point, you must move on.

Join a Local Writers Group

You will probably never find a writers' group consisting solely of those interested in writing for young adults. More likely, you will join a children's writers group that contains two or three YA writers. Or you will join an adult writers group that has one or two members who write YA material. The ideal group is one that has several published members who can offer guidance and advice. If you join a critique group where members read each other's work, the best ones usually have about five people.

Remember to take most of what is said about your work with a grain of salt. Some of the worst and most inaccurate advice comes out of critique groups. Fortunately, so does some of the best advice. A writers group should provide moral support along with information about writing. It should be a place to go for friendship and commiserating. If you find yourself always uptight and leaving with hurt feelings or anger, then by all means get out. Do not allow yourself to be subjected to such treatment. Likewise, be considerate when you critique the work of your peers. Trust your instincts. In the end, only you can decide if your work is ready for the publisher.

Join a Professional Writers Organization

This is not the same as a critique group or writers club. A professional organization is one that gives support on a national basis, often with state chapters. The Society of Children's Book Writers and Illustrators (SCBWI) is the primary organization for authors of YA literature. Based in California, it has approximately ten thousand members worldwide. There are SCBWI chapters in most states; some states have several. The benefits of joining SCBWI are many: informative publications, updated newsletters, marketing lists, contests and awards, professional advice and an annual conference in California. The local chapters hold annual conferences as well.

There are many national organizations specializing in specific genres, including Romance Writers of America, Western Writers of America, Mystery Writers of America, Horror Writers of America and Science Fiction Writers of America. These organizations also have publications, contests, conferences and local chapters.

Attend Related Conferences

The aforementioned writers organizations all hold excellent annual conferences. Almost every state has some type of annual writers conference, often sponsored by a local university. Conferences specializing in children's and YA writing are, of course, ideal. But even conferences that do not specialize in children's or YA writing can be useful to a beginner since editors from large publishing companies often attend and are able to answer general questions.

Other recommended conferences to attend are the American Library Association conferences, bookseller conventions, the National Council of Teachers of English Conference, the International Reading Association Conference, and conferences of state library associations. At these conferences, children's publishers set up booths and hand out promotional materials, including free catalogs. Editors often attend the larger conferences, and children's authors speak and sign autographs.

Network With Authors and Editors

Never pass up the opportunity to talk to an author or editor at a conference. Editors and authors are human. They're not gods and most of them don't bite. I have sold several books as a direct result of talking with editors at conferences, and these were local, rather small conferences. Most editors and authors do not mind polite, intelligent questions—just be sure to do your homework beforehand. For example, read something the author has written or know what the editor's publishing house has published. Prove to them that you are serious about becoming an author.

Never, never, never ask an author or editor to read a manuscript that you just happen to have in your briefcase. I cannot count the number of times I have visited a school, spoken at a conference or participated in a book signing, only to have a parent, student or novice writer hold out a manuscript (or an illustration) and ask me to critique it in my spare time. First, authors and editors have no spare time. Second, there are professionals who get paid to do just that. Such a request would be like meeting a dentist at a party and asking him to repair your broken tooth in his spare time. Be polite and professional, and the editor will remember you when you send in that manuscript, or the author will share some great advice.

Subscribe to Writers Magazines and Read How-To Books

Since you are reading this book, you are already on your way, but there are many other resources out there. (For a comprehensive list of periodicals and reference materials, see Appendix.) Of all the magazines available, I recommend *Publishers Weekly* (PW) for keeping up with the publishing world. It has the most up-to-date news about editorial policies, changes and the rise and fall of publishing houses and imprints, as well as informative articles, best-seller lists and reviews. *PW* is very expensive; however, you can find copies at most public libraries.

I also recommend that you become familiar with the main review sources for YA literature, such as *School Library Journal*, *Booklist* and *The Horn Book* (see Appendix for a list of sources). Unlike the adult publishing field, reviews are critical to the success of hardcover children's books.

◆ ◆ ◆

At last, you have set writing goals, established a writing area, are motivated and have familiarized yourself with the YA category and the writing industry. Whether you decide to write a 500-word picture book, a nonfiction book about acne or a young adult novel, all books begin in the same way—with an idea.

Chapter Eight

Step Two: Visit the Idea Tree

As I travel to schools across the country speaking to children and young adults, I always leave plenty of time in my presentation for the audience to ask questions. Almost without exception, someone will ask: "Where do you get your ideas?"

Nonwriters seem to think that authors have a direct telephone line with spirits or aliens, that we see and hear invisible things floating in the air. They also seem to think that once one author has picked an idea from the idea tree, no one else may ever use it again. Some nonwriters think that getting an idea for a book is so difficult that they must share their own ideas with you, as if you would otherwise have none. However, finding ideas for books is actually the easiest part of being an author. I don't know any successful author who doesn't have an idea file jammed with plans for future books. As a matter of fact, most authors I know are not concerned with where the next idea for a book will come from, but where they will ever find the *time* to write all those books.

So the truthful answer to the question "Where do you get your ideas" is "Everywhere." Everything you see, hear and do, and every person you meet, becomes potential grist for the mill. To be more specific, here are the main sources for ideas.

Written Sources

Newspapers, nonfiction books, novels, periodicals, diaries, journals, the Bible, Shakespeare, mythology, billboards, cereal boxes and birthday cards are examples of written sources. If you write historical fiction, most of your ideas will come from some bit of history you read, often in a dusty, obscure tome. I got the idea to write *Indio*, a YA novel set in 1500s Mexico, while doing research for a contemporary book set in a Texas ghost town. I was inspired to write *Song of the Buffalo Boy*, a YA novel about Amerasians in Vietnam, after reading an article in *Parade Magazine*. Newspapers are great sources for contemporary novels that deal with modern adolescent problems.

Audiovisual Sources

Television, movies, radio and the observation of others are audiovisual sources. Whether we like it or not, television is one of the most powerful influences in modern society. Many authors of contemporary novels get material from the evening news, which abounds with gripping stories. I wrote *I Never Knew Your Name*, a book about teen suicide, after hearing a story on the six o'clock news about several local teens who had killed themselves. I wrote *Letters From the Mountain* after watching a documentary and reading newspaper articles about teenagers who "huffed" toxic inhalants and suffered brain damage. PBS and cable channels that specialize in documentaries and educational programs are a tremendous source for both fiction and nonfiction ideas.

People You Meet

Sometimes you meet an individual with such an interesting occupation, personality or life experience that you just need to incorporate that person's experiences into a story. For me, it was a wrong phone number—a talkative, intoxicated man who said he used to be the veterinarian for the mounted police horses in the town where I live. He mentioned that local teens often volunteered after school to groom and exercise the horses. An idea for a story immediately popped into my head. A few months later, at a park opening, I observed that a police officer and his horse were the main attraction, so I talked to the officer, found out about the selection process and training of police horses, and accepted his invitation to visit the stables and do research. The end result was my middle-grade novel *Best Horse on the Force*.

Personal Experiences

Kids often ask me if my stories are based on things that really happened to me, and are disappointed to learn that I lead an ordinary life. I wasn't raised in China, nor did I run away from home as a teen or fight bulls in Spain. As a matter of fact, one of the main reasons I did not attempt to write novels until I was over thirty was that I didn't think I had experienced life enough to say anything profound.

But sometimes events that may not seem significant at the time will turn out to be the inspiration for a novel. In my case, it was meeting a Vietnamese family in 1981. As I became close friends with this family, and then many other Vietnamese families, I had no idea that someday their lives and personal tragedies and triumphs would be the most influential force in my writing career. Yet that's what happened. Because of my close association with Vietnamese families, I turned to writing about Vietnam. *Shadow of the Dragon* is set in contemporary Houston and focuses on the struggle of a Vietnamese-American teenager trying to balance two cultures. Many of the novel's scenes are derived from actual events that I observed or participated in.

Titles

Oddly enough, many authors, myself included, think of titles first—perhaps a quote from a book, a line from a poem or a catchy phrase. Then they begin to search for the perfect plot to go along with that great title.

Thin Air

I personally do not believe that ideas appear out of thin air. I believe that something heard, read or experienced triggers an idea. But there are those who claim that the idea hit them from out of the blue. Other authors may get ideas from their dreams. My first novel—a long historical that still sits boxed in the closet—emerged that way.

WRITE IT DOWN IMMEDIATELY

Once you have an idea, no matter what the source, it is very important to get it on paper (or into a computer file). I cannot begin to tell you how many times I have thought of great stories while driving, drifting off to sleep at night or in the middle of watching a movie or TV program. I always tell myself that I won't forget this one, but I always do. Unless you have a photographic memory, chances are that you will, too. Keep a notepad and pen or a tape recorder within reach in the house or car, your handbag or shirt pocket. Write whatever thoughts you have about the idea, plot and characters to help jar your memory the next time you see your notes.

KEEP AN IDEA FILE

Collecting ideas is like collecting pretty stones and placing them in a jar. Some of them will turn out to be too rough to polish into stones for rings, bracelets or necklaces, but others, after reshaping and buffing, will become beautiful jewelry. The point behind an idea file is that nothing is too silly, stupid or crazy to put into it. Some of the ideas will be forgotten within a few days, others will demand to be put on paper right away, and still others will quietly haunt you for weeks, months or years. Some authors file their ideas on note cards arranged by topics.

START WITH WHAT YOU KNOW

The old axiom "Write what you know" is good advice in many ways. The best writing seems to come from authors who write about their hometown or personal experiences. If you are stuck for an idea, try making a list of everything you know something about:

- hobbies and special interests
- places you have lived or visited
- careers you have had
- experiences you or someone you know have had
- events that happened in your locality, past or present
- interesting people you know

Brainstorm, listing as many items as you are able, and then think of ideas for articles or books.

For example, a hurricane passed over my house in 1983, leaving an image emblazoned on my mind and in my heart. Coincidentally, I live about fifty miles from romantic, historical Galveston Island, which suffered the worst natural disaster in American history—the Hurricane of 1900, which killed over six thousand people. On visits to Galveston, I always enjoyed the ocean, and have noticed a couple of horse stables established along the beach for tourists. Loving horses and Galveston, as well as living through a hurricane, all combined to form my YA novel *The Silent Storm*, which has received several honors.

WHICH IDEAS TO DEVELOP?

When determining which ideas to develop, ask yourself, "Will I still be interested in this idea one year from now?" Every book, whether fiction or nonfiction, will require a certain amount of research and revision. You should be certain that you will maintain your interest in the topic throughout the duration of the research, first drafts, revisions, polishing and, if you sell it, the editing and rewriting phases.

The whole process for a YA novel can easily take a couple of years; nonfiction often takes longer. The research alone for *Song of the Buffalo Boy* took over two years. The writing and revisions took another year. If I had not cared about the subject of the story, I would have experienced burnout long before the revisions arrived at my door. To face the task of writing a book you're no longer interested in is not only painful and excruciating, but also too much like a "real" job to be enjoyable.

After experimenting, you will eventually learn which ideas do not work for you. With fiction, it may take a while to warm up to the story, so you begin by getting to know the characters. With nonfiction, it is important to do a quick market survey to find out if the topic is overdone or timely. (See chapter seven for an in-depth discussion of nonfiction.)

It's okay to be dissatisfied with certain parts of your projects, to run into stumbling blocks here and there; but, if you struggle endlessly with the story or find that you do not like the characters, setting or plot, you should probably put that project back into your idea file. Maybe you just aren't ready for it. Maybe you need a bit more experience. All authors have projects "in the drawer"—work that never blossomed into salable material. Do not think of those projects as failures, but as practice pieces.

When you have a terrific idea for a book, one you are willing to stick with, you are usually eager to begin. You are excited about the possibilities, but where to go from there depends on what you want to accomplish and what you want your readers to take from your book. Let's say that your sixty-five-year-old uncle's hobby is making arrowheads. He collects his own flint from the mountains and chips the heads the same way North

American Indians did. He teaches classes in arrowhead-making at a local state park and sells his handiwork at the park gift shop and at trade shows across the southwest.

You know that you want to include arrowhead-making techniques in your writing for young adults. Knowing what category you want to write will help determine how the information will be used. Do you want to teach adolescents how to make arrowheads? If so, you will probably write a nonfiction instructional book. Do you want the adolescents to have a fast-paced, entertaining story? You may want to write a mystery in which one of the uncle's arrowheads is found embedded in a dead park ranger's back, the uncle accused of murder. Do you prefer a hardcover, literary coming-of-age story? Your story, in that case, might be set in a pre-Columbian Indian village in which one boy makes his own arrowheads in preparation for his first kill. These are just a few of the many possibilities. Like the seed of a dandelion blown by the wind, each idea has many possible landings and outcomes.

Whatever idea you ultimately choose, your next step is research.

Chapter Nine

Step Three: Research Your Subject

A t a writers conference not long ago, I met an author who loudly proclaimed that she wrote only contemporary young adult novels because she hated research. Yet I know that she *does* research background material for her novels. Once she interviewed a doctor because one of her characters had an unusual disease; another time, she attended a high school pep rally to record the words of cheers and to study the cheerleaders' costumes. To the author it may not have seemed like research, but it was. And almost every writing project, whether nonfiction, fiction, historical, contemporary or short magazine pieces, requires some kind of background investigation.

GET ORGANIZED

Before tearing off to the nearest library or dropping in on the local museum, you will save tremendous amounts of time by taking a few days to get organized. Research, itself, is only as good as your organizational skills. No matter how many accurate, complete notes you take, if you cannot retrieve the information, it is useless. When I first started writing historical fiction, I relied on yellow legal pads for all my research notes. I would sit in the library or at the kitchen table taking long, copious passages from each musty volume. After months of research, or perhaps even years, I would start my novel only to find that my notes were useless. When I needed to know a specific date, word or bit of information, I found myself having to reread page after page of scribbled handwriting.

Note cards are more practical than writing pads, especially for nonfiction, when you must have information at your fingertips and where a bibliography is required. Make a separate note card for each reference source. At the top of the card print the subject followed by the title, author, date, publisher and town, and page numbers. If your source is a periodical, be sure to include the volume and issue numbers. Finally, write any pertinent notes for later reference. If the book came from the library, also write down the call number in case you must refer to it again.

As you accumulate cards, start grouping them by subject. For nonfiction, divide the cards by chapter into separate file folders or separate with dividers in an index card box. For a fiction project that yields a large amount of notes, you may want to label file folders by subject matter. And if you have a lot of material other than notes—books, clippings, maps, photos, tapes and artifacts—try keeping them all together in a large cardboard storage box. My nonfiction book about Vietnam had so many pieces of material that I bought a filing cabinet for them.

Tape recorders are used by many authors to record their impressions while carrying out on-site research or personal interviews. Some people don't like to be taped and become very self-conscious, so if you use a recorder for an interview, ask for the interviewee's permission first.

A **library card** is a necessity as research requires repeated trips to the public library. And don't overlook university libraries. Many will issue cards to non-students for a fee. Other libraries can be found within large companies, hospitals, associations and private organizations.

A **camera** will help when doing firsthand research. For nonfiction, photographs are essential. But even with fiction, a photograph can help to describe a location, person or artifact. While researching *Indio*, which is set in the region along the Texas–Mexico border, I visited the area three times. Of course, the indigenous people who farmed there long ago are extinct, but I needed to know what the plants, river and land looked like. Expecting rugged terrain of mountains and canyons, I was flabbergasted to discover that the exact spot I had selected was a small, flat area of riverine plain. That ruined all of my scenes, so I relocated to the village farther up the Rio Grande in a more mountainous region. I crossed over the border into Mexico and took several rolls of film. When later writing descriptions of the area, I kept some of the photos in front of me for accuracy and inspiration.

The first challenge to a researcher is where to find the necessary materials. Research resources can be divided into two main categories, primary and secondary. The type of book you are writing will determine what kind of research you must do.

PRIMARY SOURCES

Obviously, not all research involves studying reference books. Primary sources of research involve going directly to the source, whether that source comes from your own personal experiences, an interview, or actual diaries, journals or letters. Primary research can be as much, or even more, fun than writing the book itself. Let's take a closer look at each type of primary source.

Personal experiences. Your experiences have the ability to make your work sparkle with detail. That is why so many authors write books that focus on people, occupations or locations they know well. If possible, travel to your novel's setting. Take notes (and photographs where applicable) about the climate, geology, flora, fauna, man-made structures, clothing, hairstyles, food, festivals, customs and amusements. Do what your hero or heroine will do: Swim in the ocean, dig for clams, play a game of pool, climb a mountain or roll in the snow. Pay attention to sensory experiences. Smell the air. Listen to the sounds of the streets, the insects or the vendors. Eat local food, especially those you are not familiar with. Touch the hump on a buffalo's back.

The YA novel for which I did the most firsthand research was *The Silent Storm*, set on Galveston Island at the time of a hurricane. Yes, I was in a hurricane, and no, not by choice. It happened in 1983 while I was struggling with the then-untitled novel. Hurricane Alicia was small, but as it raged, I ran outside and let the wind and rain hit my face. And when the eye of the storm passed over, I went outside again and saw the moon and stars in a clear sky. I sloshed through flooded streets where neighbors paddled around in boats. After the storm was over, I drove to Galveston Island and looked at the damage done to the houses, shops and landscape.

Alyssa, the heroine of *The Silent Storm*, helps her ailing grandfather with his horse rental business along the beach, so I visited a stable, rented a horse and rode along the beach with the wind and rain in my face. I also needed to learn about flounder fishing, so I grabbed some fishing poles and set off with some friends. We did catch a flounder and although it was by accident, it was the experience that counted: the smell of the bait, the slap of the waves, the whine of the fishing reel and the tug on the line. I camped out on the beach and observed the wildlife. And, of course, I shot many rolls of film—pictures of everything and everyone I saw. Every moment was exciting and enjoyable. Here is how a bit of that research looked after being turned into prose:

> Little ghost crabs scurried like shadows across her path as Alyssa crept along, trying not to stumble over the wild buttercups and tangy-smelling bindweed that covered the ground. They were on the leeward side of Galveston island, so there were no big ocean waves. It was peaceful and quiet, except for the laughing sea gulls overhead and the soft lap of the inland waves from the bay.

Interviews. There are two types of interviews, formal and informal. The *formal interview* is most often used when the subject of the interview is someone you are writing about (for a biography) or an expert on something related to your topic. For example, if your hero's father suffered a heart attack, you might interview a heart surgeon. For the formal interview, you either call or write in advance to set an interview time. If the person lives far away, a phone interview will suffice. You may also interview famous personalities by mail, but that is riskier, because you may not get a quick reply. In your initial letter or phone call, explain who you are and that you are writing a book for children. Those magical words open untold doors. I have never met anyone who was not willing to give a few moments to an author writing for children. Explain how the interview information will be used (for example, if it is for fiction, describe the scene).

Prepare well-thought-out questions in advance. You should have already done enough background research to know the basic facts about the topic or person. Don't waste time on questions for which you know the answers to or can find in other resources. You are looking for firsthand experiences and unusual or interesting facts. Be prompt. Never tape-record without permission. When interviewing in person, maintain eye contact. If taking notes, don't scribble furiously, writing every word said. Instead, write key words or use shorthand, unless you are going to use the sentence as a direct quote, in which case you must be accurate. Type your notes into a readable format while they are still fresh in your mind. And if you do decide to quote the person, always double-check with him or her for accuracy before the book is published.

Send a thank-you note. It is not customary to pay for interviews or to give the interviewee royalties. However, if the interviewee insists on royalties, it is best to select another person. Do, however, give the interviewee credit somewhere in your book (usually in the acknowledgment section), and a free copy of the published work.

The *informal interview* is one for which you do not make an appointment. These interviews usually occur on the spur of the moment when you need information and anyone with knowledge on the subject will do. For example, one of the characters in *The Silent Storm* works on his stepfather's shrimp boat, so I spoke to some shrimp boat captains on Galveston Island, asked dozens of questions, and went out on one of the boats and even fished from the stern. None of this was planned ahead of time. I just walked out onto the docks and began talking with shrimpers after explaining that I was writing a children's book. I asked very specific questions: What time of day do you leave and return? What do those blinking red lights mean? How do you radio for help in an emergency? Where do you take the boat when a hurricane hits? I acknowledged the shrimper who helped me the most, and later gave him a complimentary copy.

Informal interviews can be the most interesting and rewarding. To break the ice, smile friendly and say something like: "Hello, my name is Jane Smythe. I'm writing a children's book about a boy whose father is a shrimper on the Gulf Coast. Do you know anyone who would be able to answer a few questions about shrimp boats?" If the person does not have knowledge of the topic, he or she will usually refer you to someone who does, perhaps even an expert, either by profession or by hobby. This is the joy of research, never knowing what undiscovered treasure lies ahead.

For more in-depth advice on interviewing, consult *The Craft of Interviewing* by John Brady or *Interviewing Children and Adolescents* by John Rich.

Diaries, letters, journals and speeches. If you are writing about a historical person, place or event, a diary, journal, letter or speech can be as valuable as an interview. You can assume that the feelings expressed in a diary are the writer's true feelings. In a biography about a historical personage, you cannot make up dialogue, but you may quote from letters as if the words had been spoken. For example, in her book *I Am Houston*, biographer Mary Dodson Wade quoted from a letter written by General Sam Houston after his victory over Santa Anna at the Battle of San Jacinto. In one paragraph she captures the personality of Houston:

> Houston collapsed and was laid under an oak tree. While a doctor treated his shattered ankle, he arranged three magnolia leaves and wrote a note to Anna Raguet in Nacogdoches: "These are laurels I send you from the battlefield of San Jacinto. Thine, Houston."

Not only are diaries, journals and letters extremely invaluable to biographers, but they are also good sources of information about the culture and customs of a specific time period. A diary or letter may make reference to a popular song, a style of a woman's hat or a local politician. It may reveal small incidents that other sources do not, and it will reveal the style of the language for that time period.

Where can you find diaries? The reference book *American Diaries: An Annotated Bibliography of Published American Diaries and Journals*, edited by Laura Arksey, is a good source, as are *American Diaries in Manuscript, 1580–1954* by William Matthews and *And So to Bed: A Bibliography of Diaries Published in English* by Patricia Havlice. For an extensive list of reference books about primary sources, consult the research section of *Children's Writer Guide* (see Appendix).

Period newspapers and publications. Period newspapers are good sources for language style, moral values and general social situations within a historical period. Nearly every fair-sized town in America and Europe had a newspaper, and reading those papers today can be a great source of knowledge and entertainment. However, when it comes to the accuracy of historical events and quotations, newspapers can be unreliable. Within a month after the fall of the Alamo, there were dozens of varying accounts circulating in newspapers and, to this day, the actual events are not completely known. Quotations should not be taken from a period newspaper unless they can be verified by other reputable sources; journalists in the past were notorious for embellishing historical events, especially those that occurred in remote areas.

Other periodicals which can be extremely useful for historical novels are period magazines and manufacturers' catalogs. If you need to know the kinds of washing machines available to housewives in 1891 or want to get an idea of the styles of women's corsets or men's shoes, check an 1891 *Sears Roebuck Catalog*. If you want to know what women were interested in or what recipes were popular, read old issues of *The Ladies' Home Companion* or *Harper's Weekly*. Almanacs and instructional books often describe planting procedures or new products in great detail. These periodicals also list prices, so you can be realistic when money changes hands in your novel.

SECONDARY SOURCES

Although some authors get by using only primary sources for their research, most need to consult secondary sources—written materials, audiovisual materials and the Internet. Secondary sources are abundant and can seem overwhelming, but with a systematic approach, you will do just fine.

Start at the Library

Compile a bibliography of sources. Start with the most obvious: *Books in Print*. If your topic is popular, you may find several pages of possible sources. (If your library does not have a *Books in Print*, check with a local bookstore.) Other lists of books can be found in *The Cumulative Book Index* (books printed since 1898) and *Guide to Reference Books*. Books that list libraries include the *American Library Directory* and *Subject Collection: A Guide to Special Libraries*.

Another way to begin your bibliography is to consult encyclopedias. Locate your topic's entry; it may be very short, but it will list other books and related topics. As you look up the topics in the encyclopedias, keep a list of books mentioned in the text and bibliography.

As you consult each book, be sure to make a copy of the bibliography even if you find a book that is not helpful. Also, pay attention to footnotes; sometimes they include information and reference sources not mentioned in the bibliography. Each time you read a new book, you will probably find one or two new reference sources. Remember to check the children's section, too. Even though the books are written for children, the bibliographies often list adult reference books. The mail-order book dealer, Gryphon Books, specializes in reference books for writers. To receive their catalog, write to: Gryphon Books, P.O. Box 926, Hernando, MS 38632.

Often one source will quickly lead to another. For example, you may find a book in print written by John Smythe, look it up in the card catalog (or online) and discover that he also wrote several older books on the same topic that are no longer in print. Browsing through relevant sections of the library (or bookstore) may also uncover good sources not on your original list.

Interlibrary loan. This is a source often overlooked by novice researchers. If you know of a book that your local public library, the college library and local bookstore do not possess, do not give up. Most libraries offer a service called *Interlibrary Loan* (ILL). After placing your request with the ILL librarian, she will perform a computer search for the nearest library that holds a copy of the book. Often this can be done while you wait, or within one day. The librarian will inform you of where the nearest copy is located. You may decide to drive there yourself, or the ILL librarian may contact the library to borrow the book for you. Once it arrives, you will pick it up at your local library and check it out on your library card. Most libraries charge little or no fee for this service. It does, however, take time. A public library in a very large town often has so many ILL requests that it takes several weeks for the book to arrive.

Periodicals. I paid for six years of college by working in the periodical section of a university library, and spent many hours helping students find information for their research papers. I am always amazed to find that many beginning authors do not consult periodicals at all. Periodical articles are frequently very specific and written by experts in the field. They often contain a bibliography of other articles or books. *The Reader's Guide to Periodical Literature*, which is available in most libraries, lists articles that appeared in magazines from 1900 to the present. Educational articles are indexed in the Educational Resources Information Center (ERIC). There are also specific indexes for science and social studies. *Poole's Index to Periodical Literature* covers articles written between 1802 and 1906. Be sure to consult all of these sources, because you never know when a topic may appear in one of them. For example, an article about the use of anesthesia during the Civil War may appear in a medical journal.

Newspapers. Newspapers are also indexed. For example, the *New York Times Index* dates back to 1851 and the *London Times Index* dates back to 1790. For smaller newspapers, you may need to consult the town's library. Newspapers are especially helpful if you are writing historical fiction, for they reflect customs, clothing styles, language and society as a whole. As mentioned before, though, be very cautious when quoting from an old newspaper. They are sometimes unreliable when it comes to facts about events.

Visit Museums and Archives

For historical researchers, much information can be gleaned from archives, which are often stored in universities. Some of the material is original and too delicate to be handled, but in many cases it has been reprinted in book form. Museum bookstores sell material related to the contents of the museum, and often these books are hard to find elsewhere.

Contact Organizations, Associations and Agencies

All of these groups have publications related to their field of interest. I have already mentioned the bountiful sources of government agencies which print reams of publications and keep millions of photographs. Historical associations and genealogical societies usually have their own journals containing articles related to the surrounding area; foundations print material related to their expertise; and organizations, even large companies, often have material that is free for the asking. For example, I picked up a free booklet entitled *More H.E.L.P.—How to Enjoy Living With a Preadolescent*, published by the National Middle

School Association. The booklet contains information about the traits of adolescents and the changes they go through.

Use Audiovisual Materials

Today's authors have research sources not available to writers fifty years ago. Included in this category is television. TV-magazine programs such as *60 Minutes* and *Dateline*, documentaries and special news broadcasts often contain a tremendous amount of material about contemporary issues. Public television, radio and some all-talk radio stations, as well as cable channels that specialize in history, nature, science or social issues, all present information in an interesting and usually accurate way. And an interview on TV or radio can be as good as an interview you have conducted yourself. Many video stores carry educational programs that were originally broadcast on PBS, and local TV stations keep a video library of broadcasts they have produced, from news programs to documentaries. Video stores (and many bookstores) have books that list available videos. Look in the subject index under your category.

One warning, however: Always avoid accounts of events that have been fictionalized for movies and made-for-television movies. Quotes, persons, events and dates from such fictionalized versions are not reliable.

Use Internet Resources

The Internet is a modern miracle. It's fantastic and it's confusing. If you're like me, you suspect that the answer to every question known to mankind is drifting somewhere in cyberspace; the problem is how to retrieve it!

In a nutshell, the Internet is a system by which telephone lines connect computers and allowing Internet users to communicate and exchange information. You connect to the Internet via a modem hooked up to your computer (the faster your computer and modem, the faster you'll be able to retrieve information). Libraries, organizations, institutions, government agencies and even individuals all have the potential to display information on the Internet in places called *Web sites*. A Web site may be as brief as one "page," or it may contain millions of pieces of information on numerous pages. For example, the Library of Congress's Web site lists information about itself and how to use its resources. Amazon.com (an on-line bookstore) has a Web site listing two-and-a-half million books for sale, plus reviews of the books and other information.

Many individual authors and illustrators have Web sites that list their books or show illustrations, provide reviews and more.

To gain access to the Internet, you must pay a *service provider.* Some charge you by the hour while others charge a flat monthly fee for unlimited use. Three of the largest servers are Compuserve, America Online (AOL) and MSNetwork. All Internet service providers can connect you to chat rooms and downloadable resources available on the Internet. The large services such as Compuserve, AOL and MSNetwork have additional chat rooms and other content specifically for their subscribers. For example, AOL provides access to encyclopedias, weather, travel, news, bulletin boards that allow you to post information for others to read, and chat rooms that allow you to communicate live with others on a specific topic. There are many chat rooms and bulletin boards where writers may share their experiences.

Once connected to the Internet, if you do not have the URL (Web address) of the Web site you want, you will need to use a search engine to find it, such as Excite, Lycos, AltaVista, Yahoo or InfoSeek. Large service providers, such as AOL, have their own search engines. Once you have called up the search engine, type in the subject matter you are interested in a box that is usually labeled *Find.* The engine will then search the Internet and create a list of Web sites that match your subject. The more specific your wording, the better. For example, if you type the word *coffee* you will not only pull up Web sites about the coffee plant and coffee beans, but also people named Coffee and coffee companies.

Remember that material on the Internet is copyrighted. You must obtain permission before quoting lengthy passages, such as interviews or excerpts from works of fiction. (See Appendix for a list of Web sites of interest to children's authors.)

Researching Teenagers

To write about young adults, you need to know something about them. This is particularly true for contemporary YA fiction. If you do not have any teenagers in your immediate family, don't fret—adolescents are everywhere.

Volunteer work. One of the best ways to come in contact with teens is to do volunteer work at local junior high or high schools, usually in the library. Be sure you are there during lunch breaks to observe the stampede, the conversations and the little dramas going on all around. While in the school, stop by the cafeteria; you may be surprised to see buffets and salad bars, frozen yogurt machines, juice and soft drink dispensers and candy machines. Walk the halls when classes are changing to get a feel for the atmosphere around lockers. Volunteer to help chaperone a school party, the prom or other school functions. Volunteer to take a group of teens (relatives, a church group or neighbors) on a local outing to a museum or amusement park, fishing, camping or to the beach (hopefully, some of the parents will come along to help). Volunteer to work at homeless shelters for teens. (Note: When taking young people on outings, be sure to get permission from the parents [in writing or in person, since teens have been known to say they have permission when they really don't] and explain that you are doing research for a novel.)

Attend school events. When was the last time you attended a high school football game? It's a great place for observing clothing, hairstyles, cliques, dating rituals, cheerleaders and parent–child interaction. Attending a school dance or the prom can uncover a motherlode of information. If you attend pep rallies and assemblies, sit near the student section rather than with the adults. Public school performances such as plays and concerts are also great places to observe teens.

Visit teen hangouts. Go to malls, game rooms, pizza parlors, skating rinks, movies, amusement parks and hamburger joints, or to the beach. Depending on your age, you may even be able to blend in and not be noticed.

Attend your high school reunion. Oh, the agony! Your high school reunion will instantly transport you back to the world of pecking orders and cliques. It will bring back a flood of memories and remind you what it was like to be a teenager. And you may find that things have not changed: The middle-aged cheerleaders and bald-headed quarterbacks may still be the popular ones, and the studious nerds may still be on the outside looking in—no matter if the nerds are now owners of computer companies, and the cheerleaders are on their fourth marriage!

Sit in on a class. Ask a teacher if you may sit in the back of the room and observe. Most will be happy to oblige. Even though the halls and rooms are filled with giants (kids seem bigger today), you'll be amazed by the flood of memories that will wash over you. Take notes not only about what you are observing, but about your emotions as well.

When to Stop

If you hate to research, you will probably complete it within a few weeks—or you'll write the kinds of books that require little research to begin with. But if you discover that you love to research, you may find yourself still buried knee-deep in books after one or two years. There comes a time, however, when you must stop and start the writing. If you have already signed a contract, that should be motivation enough. I usually know it is time to stop when the characters of the novel start screaming for attention—when I am reading about a historical incident and can actually see my fictitious characters taking part in the event.

Although background details are crucial to a novel, you must acknowledge that any novel, even a historical one, relies far more on character and plot than on researched facts. Your characters and their story must be strong and interesting enough so that the background material does not overshadow them. Once you acknowledge that it's okay not to know everything before you start writing, you will be ready to move on.

Chapter Ten

Step Four: Get Ready to Write

I f an idea suddenly comes to you, you may be tempted to run to the computer or typewriter and type out an entire chapter without pause. That is fine for individual scenes or for brainstorming an idea, but, in the long run, it is better to resist the temptation to write an entire novel without a lot of forethought.

CHARACTER-DRIVEN VS. PLOT-DRIVEN NOVELS

Some authors create a character and the story develops from that character's personality. These are called *character-driven* novels. In this type of novel the characters are so strong that the story could not exist without them. Katherine Paterson's Newbery Award-winning book, *Jacob Have I Loved*, is a good example of a character-driven book. The plot is little more than memories of events strung together, but the depth of the character portrayals makes the book outstanding.

Often, series detective novels fall into this category. Readers buy these books because they love the protagonist; it does not matter so much what the particular mystery is, as long as the hero is in it. Can you imagine one of the Sherlock Holmes stories using a different character?

Other authors begin with a plot and then create characters to fit the story. These are called *plot-driven* novels. The author may outline the entire story with no names for the characters. In these stories the plot drives the character, the plot is almost a character itself and, in many instances, the hero or heroine could be replaced by a different character with virtually no impact on the story. Some disaster novels fall into this category. During a disaster such as an earthquake, it doesn't matter who is in jeopardy or who saves the victim—the earthquake itself is the focus of the story. The books in the Goosebumps series are plot-driven novels. The horror in the stories is more important than the character who experiences it.

Many of the best novels not only have strong characters but also strong plots, and the two aspects are so interwoven that neither can be separated from the other. But whether your novel is character or plot driven, before you begin writing you must face certain preliminary questions. Some of the answers will come easily and almost subconsciously; others will take more thought and preparation.

SHOULD YOU OUTLINE YOUR NOVEL?

There are two schools of thought regarding outlining. Those in favor of outlining point out that an outline keeps a story on track. The outline, they say, gets your ideas down on paper before you can forget them.

Opponents of the outline claim that it restricts creativity. These authors say they do not know what is going to happen next any more than the hero does. In their eyes, forgoing an outline makes the writing process more exciting and enjoyable, thus eliminating writer's block.

Both schools are right; their claims are true, so you must decide what works best for you. I did not outline my first two novels. I felt totally free and enjoyed writing more than I ever had, before or since. Of course, both manuscripts ended up being very long—one having over a thousand pages. And in spite of the pleasure I derived, neither of those manuscripts sold. After that, I started outlining. Since then, every novel I have sold to publishers has been bought on the basis of an outline and sample chapters.

In my experience, having an outline—no matter how loosely structured—can be helpful when starting to write. Even those who claim they do not outline on paper probably have an outline in their heads—they know how the story will begin and end, and more or less what will happen in between.

If you decide to outline your novel before writing it, remember this: Your outline is not etched in stone. You may change it as the plot requires. The purpose of the outline is to provide direction, to prevent straying too far from the plot and from allowing secondary characters to steal the lead from the protagonist. However, if the outline does not work, scratch it and try a different approach. Your novel's outline should never stifle your creativity. (Note: This is not true of a nonfiction outline, as described in chapter six. Nonfiction outlines are complete and are rarely overhauled once they are approved by the editor. Changes in a nonfiction outline should be submitted to the editor.)

WHAT ABOUT THE TITLE?

For some authors, the title comes first, in a sudden burst of brilliance, and the story comes later. Other authors complete the entire manuscript without a title and might even let the editor select a name. Writing with a title in mind may help to keep you on track. A good title will catch the reader's eye before anything else, especially if the book is on a library shelf or squeezed in between hundreds of other YA novels in a bookstore. (The second thing the reader notices is the book cover, but its design is usually out of your hands.)

A striking title may encourage the reader to borrow or purchase the book in spite of a not-so-great blurb on the jacket; a really poor title may cause the reader to put the book down in spite of a great blurb. Today's youth (and maybe adults, too) are quick to pass judgment. A complex or difficult title may go right over their heads; one that is mushy gets left behind by the guys; one that is too action-packed may be skipped over by most of the girls. In all cases, avoid words that make the reader think the story is for younger readers. This usually means words such as *little*, *kid* or *child*. Also avoid lengthy titles. Surveys indicate that a title with more than five words loses its appeal unless it is unique (e.g., *There's a Boy in the Girl's Bathroom*).

A title should reflect the plot, a character or some aspect of the story, yet it should be unique in itself. It should evoke feelings, stir curiosity and give a hint of the story. If a story is humorous, the title should bring a smile to the lips. If it is a murder mystery, the title should make the reader think of dark and deadly things. Certain words connote female or male readership. For example, girls tend to buy novels with words such as *dream* and *love* in the title; boys like words such as *weird*, *freak*, *horror* and *dragon*. Books written to appeal to both sexes often have more neutral titles, perhaps based on the name of the character or a line from a famous quote.

The title for my YA novel *The Silent Storm* came very easily. The story takes place at the time of a hurricane, so the word *storm* was obvious. And the heroine is mute, unable to speak since witnessing the death of her parents three years before. Thus, the word *storm* has a double meaning, since an internal storm rages within the heroine's head and heart as she must make life-changing decisions.

If you are having difficulty with your title, try the word association (or branching) technique. In the middle of a sheet of paper, write down a key word about the book—a location, occupation or event. Then draw lines from the central topic and write subcategories. Under each subcategory write every word that comes to mind and then branch off and create further subcategories. Write fast and furiously, listing everything, no matter how silly it may sound. Finally, begin to combine words from the different categories and subcategories. Make a sheet for each main topic that occurs in your story.

This is how I found a title for one of my YA novels. The story is set in 1900 and features a girl in a Wild West show who befriends an old Wichita Indian who was once a famous rainmaker. I made one sheet for the words *Wild West Show*, one for *Native Americans* and one for *Rain*. My original title was *The Rainmaker's Daughter*, but the plot dictated that the girl be his granddaughter, and to me *The Rainmaker's Granddaughter* didn't sound as effective. After days of brainstorming, I finally came up with a title that both my editor and I liked: *The Last Rainmaker*.

A word of caution: Editors do have the power to change your title, just as they have the right to change words. So no matter how much you love your title, be prepared to let it go. I once had a great title that had to be changed before the book went to print. The editor called and said that another of their authors had written a novel with a very similar title—a title that could not be changed because it was part of a series. It broke my heart, but after all, publishing is a business.

WHO WILL TELL THE STORY?

Unless you are writing a survival novel about a boy or girl alone in the wilderness, most stories have several characters with the potential to narrate the story. For example, let's imagine that you are writing a story about a boy and a girl who fall in love. The boy joins the army, goes off to war and is killed. And the girl's best friend is the boy's younger sister. The story's possible narrators are the boy, the girl or the younger sister.

You probably will reject the viewpoint of the boy because the story would end with his death. If you tell the story from the viewpoint of the girl, you will almost certainly have to include scenes of physical attraction and perhaps even lovemaking; when they are apart, the reader will not know what the boy is thinking or feeling. For this type of story, knowing what both characters feel is important, so you may reject the girl's viewpoint. This leaves the sister. She is a good choice not only because she can reveal how the boy (her brother) reacts to certain situations, but also how the girl (her best friend) feels since they confide in one another. The reader has insight to all sides of the story and will know what happens even after the boy dies. This is the *narrator* style, and it is usually written in the first person point of view. (Hint: If you find your story isn't flowing, try switching the narrating role to a different character.)

WHICH POINT OF VIEW WILL YOU USE?

Once you know who will narrate the story you must decide how the story will be told. In other words, which point of view (POV) will you use? The two viewpoints used in fiction are first person and third person.

First Person POV

In first person novels, an *I* tells the story. There are two types of first person stories. In first person narrative POV, the *I* character relates someone else's story. The narrator may have her own story, too, which will be interwoven with the central plot. This narrative point of view can create a feeling of distance, which gives the reader a sense of watching a play and not being involved in the action.

In other books, the *I* is telling his own story rather than someone else's. This POV has the advantage of immediately placing the reader into the action and emotions of the hero. The senses and emotions are more obvious, since the narrator can simply make statements that will be taken as truth. The hero can tell, rather than show. For example, he may blatantly state: "I hate the math teacher!" Usually, children easily identify with the first person protagonist. The disadvantages come with the limits placed on this point of view. Descriptions of people, places and things are limited, because a narrator would not describe those things around him with which he is already familiar. The other characters' feelings can only be expressed through their actions or dialogue. Only what the narrator sees, hears or reads can be used. Some examples of excellent first person YA novels are *Jacob Have I Loved* by Katherine Paterson, *Fallen Angels* by Walter Dean Myers and S.E. Hinton's books *The Outsiders* and *That Was Then, This is Now.*

The first person *diary* format is gaining in popularity. There are now entire series written in the format of diaries. A diary combines elements of both narrator and main protagonist POVs. There are entries in which the diary writer talks about her own experiences and feelings, and also entries where she narrates events that happened to someone else and records their feelings. The diary format is very challenging and, in many ways, more difficult to write than a standard novel. The diary may appear to be a series of unrelated daily entries but, in fact, it must also have characters and a plot. There must be an underlying story with a beginning, middle and end, but it must be written with little dialogue and description. All of the books in Scholastic's new series Dear America are written in the diary format.

Third Person POV

The most commonly used POV in today's literature is *third person limited*. Though the story is still seen through the eyes of the main protagonist, *I* is replaced with *he, she* or the protagonist's name. The readers must now draw their own conclusions about how the protagonist feels, as seen in his actions and reactions, dialogue and, more rarely, internal thought. The following passage illustrates use of the third person to convey the meaning of the previous example, "I hate the math teacher!"

Brandon felt the heat rising to his cheeks when he saw the math teacher coming down the hall. He clenched his fists and glared as Mr. Brown passed by the lockers, whistling the same tune he did every time he gave an algebra test.

"Someday I'm going to shove that stupid tune down his throat," Brandon whispered to Sally.

In other words, the author must *show* rather than *tell*. Examples of good YA novels written in third person POV are *Children of the River* by Linda Crew and *Lyddie* by Katherine Paterson.

In *third person omniscient*, the author allows the reader to know what is going on in the minds of many characters, not just the hero's. Even the author's thoughts are included. This point of view, however, is rarely used in YA literature today. It was popular in the 1800s adult novels in which the author knew everything about everyone and often paused to divulge some bit of information to the reader that the protagonist didn't know. These books often gave the reader a sense of being up in a treetop looking down at something going on in a field. It's difficult to get emotional about such tiny, distant characters and events. The following passage is an example of an omniscient POV.

Too bad Brandon hated his math teacher. Mr. Brown truly liked Brandon and would have tutored him after school free of charge if only he had asked. Now Mr. Brown was forced to treat Brandon like all the other boys who cut up in class, though he knew Brandon wasn't really like them at all.

Alternating Viewpoint

Although alternating the viewpoint between characters often occurs in today's adult literature, it is rarely used in young adult novels. If you do use this device, it is recommended that the POV switch alternates from chapter to chapter, rather than within a single chapter, and never within a single scene. *The Pigman*, by Paul Zindel, is an excellent example. One chapter is told through the POV of the male protagonist; the next chapter is told from the POV of the female protagonist. When switching character viewpoints like this, the story is usually told in the first person.

It is also possible to switch from third person to first person through internal thoughts and letters or journals. This is the method that author Marj Gurasich uses in her award-winning YA historical novel *Letters From Oma*. Though the story is told in the third person, the heroine's emotions and deepest secrets are revealed through a series of first person letters sent to her grandmother in Germany.

An author should not begin a scene from one character's POV, switch midscene, and end that scene from someone else's point of view. This has been done in certain pulp fiction genres and is not only difficult for the reader to follow, but also is a sign of lazy writing. Rather than slipping into a secondary character's POV, it is better to *show* the reader what the character feels.

WHAT IS THE NOVEL'S THEME?

A novel's *theme* is the backbone that holds all the pieces together that are scattered here and there. Knowing the theme will help to keep you on track and move the story toward its conclusion. Examples of YA themes include coming of age (e.g., loss of innocence and learning about life's realities), taking responsibility for one's actions, sacrificing for the good of others, the importance of family, there's no place like home (e.g., prodigal son returns), accept yourself, you can't judge a book (or a person) by its cover, do what you know is right and help others and you help yourself. You will notice that many themes common to YA novels are the same as philosophies put forth in famous proverbs: "Do unto others . . ." and "Virtue is its own reward" to name two. That is because themes are man-made and universal; they transcend race, religion and politics. Themes involve wisdom that adults learn over a lifetime. Children's books or YA novels are one of the first places that young people are exposed to these universal themes.

A theme is not the same as a plot. *Plot* is the mechanism by which the author conveys a theme. Theme is subtle, and more than one theme may occur in a story. Think of several great YA novels and ask yourself what the themes are. In *Huckleberry Finn,* for example, the plot involves a boy and a runaway slave traveling down a river; one of the themes is "do what you know is right." The plot of *To Kill a Mockingbird* centers on the trial of a falsely accused man, but one of the themes is "don't judge a book by its cover"—the book, in this case, being Boo Radley. The plot of *Song of the Buffalo Boy* involves a seventeen-year-old Amerasian girl running away from an arranged marriage to be with the boy she loves; the theme is "accept yourself."

Whatever theme you choose, whether it is a fast-paced series book or a lofty work of literature, every novel contains basic elements. All novels have characters, a plot and use words and sentences. Part IV will concentrate on the basic elements of writing a YA novel.

PART FOUR

The Craft of Writing Young Adult Fiction

Chapter Eleven

A Grand Opening

Have you ever picked up a book while browsing in a bookstore and read the first paragraph? Have you ever put a book down because you didn't like the opening page? I have. The opening page comes after the book jacket and title page in order of importance to the YA reader.

Young readers have a limited amount of time to make book selections. In most cases, they are brought to the bookstore by a parent who has a million other things to do. In just a few minutes, the child must choose from hundreds of possibilities. One reason series books are so popular is because little thinking is involved in selecting a book: Just grab the next book in the series.

Or let's suppose a seventh-grade English teacher has instructed her students to read a YA book of their choice. Imagine that she takes the class to the library and allows them fifteen minutes to select a book and sign it out. What factors will make the student choose one novel over another? One factor is recommendation—by friends, siblings or even the teacher. Another is name recognition—famous authors of books they have already read. The third factor is appearance—title and book jacket; and the fourth is subject matter—some girls may choose stories about emotions and relationships, while some boys may choose books about adventure, war, gangs, humor or sports.

With the choices thus narrowed down, now comes the true test. The young adult begins to read the first few paragraphs to make his final selection. A great opening will make the reader want to choose that book (possibly yours) above all others. It will captivate the reader's interest and stimulate curiosity.

Curiosity will drive the young reader to want to continue reading the story. The reader may learn something while reading and feel emotions along the way, but the basic reason for turning page after page is to find out what happens next.

HOOK YOUR READERS IN THE FIRST PARAGRAPHS
Open During a Change

In many good openings, something has just happened, is happening or is about to happen to the protagonist that will disrupt his normal life. Maybe the high schooler has walked the same route every day for the entire school year, but on the last day of school he decides to take a different path and finds a dead body, meets an elf, loses his way or finds an injured dog. Sometimes the change is as major as losing a parent, moving to a new town or going to war. Sometimes the change is as minor as losing a video game for the first time or seeing a circus come to town.

As the change is revealed in the opening paragraphs, the reader may consider several questions: How is this change going to affect the protagonist's life? How is the protagonist going to get out of this mess? What will happen next? In each of the examples, the reader's curiosity has been piqued.

I must admit, this kind of opening is one of my favorites. Chapter one from *The Silent Storm* opens with:

> That steamy August morning would have been like any other except for two things: It was Alyssa MacAllister's thirteenth birthday, and she heard voices. Alyssa heard the voices long before she saw three shadowy figures sneaking through the marsh reeds along the finger-shaped cove that jutted into West Bay. The figures were searching for something, and in her heart she knew it was the green boat.

Hopefully, the reader now wants to know who the shadowy figures are, why they are looking for a green boat and why the boat so important.

Maniac Magee, the 1991 Newbery winner written by Jerry Spinelli, also opens with an impending change:

> Maniac Magee was not born in a dump. He was born in a house, a pretty ordinary house, right across the river from

here, in Bridgeport. And he had regular parents, a mother
and a father.

But not for long.

The intriguing line "But not for long" draws the reader into the
story. Something is going to happen in Maniac's life, and only
by continuing to read do you learn what that something is.

Open With an Interesting Character

Many character-driven novels open with a description or
scene that creates a character so fascinating that the reader has
no choice but to continue. S.E. Hinton's classic YA novels have
such openings. Consider the first lines of *The Outsiders*:

> When I stepped out into the bright sunlight from the
> darkness of the movie house, I had only two things on my
> mind: Paul Newman and a ride home. I was wishing I
> looked like Paul Newman—he looks tough and I don't. . . .

The opening lines from Hinton's *That Was Then, This Is Now*
are equally compelling:

> Mark and me went down to the bar/pool hall about two
> or three blocks from where we lived with the sole intention
> of making some money. We'd done that before. I was a
> really good pool player, especially for being just sixteen
> years old. . . .

In both examples, in-depth characterization compels the reader
to find out more about the protagonist.

Open With an Interesting Setting

Sometimes a setting can be so intriguing that the reader falls
under its spell. The setting may be another country, time period
or planet. The opening scene for Karen Cushman's Newbery
Award-winning novel, *The Midwife's Apprentice*, is unique and
memorable:

> When animal droppings and garbage and spoiled straw
> are piled up in a great heap, the rotting and moiling give
> forth heat. Usually no one gets close enough to notice be-
> cause of the stench. But the girl noticed and, on that frosty

night, burrowed deep into the warm, rotting muck, heed-
less of the smell. . . .

Now that is a setting that makes a reader sit up and take notice.
A more subtle opening is Scott O'Dell's *Sing Down the Moon*,
where the beauty of scenery and language immediately pull the
reader into the story.

> On the high Mesas above our canyon spring came early
> that year. The piñon trees shook off their coverings of snow
> in the month of the deer. Warm winds melted the snow and
> blue water gathered under the trees and ran through the
> meadows and down the steep barrancas. . . .

Open With Dialogue

One of the quickest ways to draw the reader into a story is
through dialogue. Some critics disapprove of this technique because it tends to be overused. Yet opening with dialogue can
be very powerful, as Walter Dean Myers's masterpiece, *Fallen
Angels*, demonstrates. Two young army recruits, on their way to
Vietnam in 1968, are speaking while the plane is refueling in
Alaska:

> "Somebody must have told them suckers I was coming."
> "Told who?" I asked.
> "The Congs, man. Who you think I'm talking 'bout?"
> "Why do you think somebody told them you were
> coming?"
> " 'Cause I don't see none of 'em around here. They don't
> want their butts kicked."
> "Yeah, okay." I looked at the guy's name tag. It read
> 'Gates.' "Hey, Gates. I'll tell you as soon as I see some
> Congs."
> "I'm going on in the bathroom," he said. "Make sure
> they ain't none in there."
> "Right."

The reader knows from this opening dialogue that the book
will contain realistic language, it is about the Vietnam War
and the narrator is a sensible, intelligent young man. The

reader cannot help but feel that the macho optimism of Gates will vanish by the end of the story, and that the novel will be poignant and moving.

Open With Humor

Young readers appreciate humor, especially those ages eleven through thirteen. Even books with a serious theme often use humor to make a point. One of the most hilarious books to come along in a long time is *Catherine, Called Birdy*, the Newbery Honor novel written by Karen Cushman. Set in the thirteenth century, it presents history in the format of a most entertaining diary kept by the fourteen-year-old daughter of an English nobleman. The first entries snare the unsuspecting reader of this thin volume:

12th Day of September—
I am commanded to write an account of my days: I am bit by fleas and plagued by family. That is all there is to say.
13th Day of September—
My father must suffer from ale head this day, for he cracked me twice before dinner instead of once. I hope his angry liver bursts.
14th Day of September—
Tangled my spinning again. Corpus bones, what a torture.

Open With an Atmospheric or Suspenseful Description

Atmosphere alone can draw a reader into the story. This is especially true of mystery, horror, suspense and gothic novels in which the feeling of impending death or crisis creates a desire to keep reading. Almost any book written by Joan Lowery Nixon, four-time Edgar Award winner for her YA mysteries, demonstrates this point. From *The Specter* comes this opening:

The whisper strikes though the darkness, and I struggle to meet it, clutching at the sound.
"Sikes!" It comes again, a terrifying hiss.

And from *The Weekend Was Murder* comes this:

A chilling silence filled the nineteenth floor of the Ridley Hotel as Tina Martinez and I stepped from the elevator into the hallway. Mutely lighted, the dark-paneled walls seemed to breathe inward, as though someone had suddenly stopped talking to listen intently. Tina nervously glanced to the right and the left and gave a little shiver.

Joan Lowery Nixon, in an on-line interview, once explained that she works on the openings of her novels for a long time, perfecting them before starting the rest of the novels. To her, the openings are one of the most important aspects of the mystery. But not all atmospheric openings belong to mystery novels. In *Indio*, the opening illustrates the atmosphere of a dark, lonely canyon, with a hint of things to come.

> Pale beams of dying moonlight fell upon the canyon path. Ipa-tah-chi knew the trail so well that her yucca-fiber sandals found the hidden notches and unseen rocks without the help of her eyes. But Ipa's younger brother, Kadoh, was only five summers old and had not climbed the path in darkness before. He stumbled, making pebbles rain to the canyon below, where flat-roofed adobe houses squatted beside the Great River.
>
> "Come, Little Brother. The top of the canyon is near," Ipa whispered as she helped her brother up and brushed a layer of red sand from his bare legs.

Curious, the reader will read on to discover why the characters are climbing the canyon wall at night and what is going to happen when they reach the top.

TRY A DRAMATIC PROLOGUE

Many authors use prologues at the beginning of their novels. The prologue is part of the story and often contains important information presented in a tantalizing way. It can serve two purposes.

When the prologue is used to foreshadow the story, it is usually told in the past tense after the events of the story have occurred. This is a throwback to the omniscient POV: The author already knows the story and is imparting some hint of the outcome. An example of this type of prologue can be found in Katherine Paterson's Newbery Award-winning book *Jacob Have I Loved*, which begins with a prologue called "Rass Island." It is written after the heroine is an adult.

> As soon as the snow melts, I will go to Rass and fetch my mother. At Crisfield I'll board the ferry, climbing down into the cabin where the women always ride, but after forty minutes of sitting on the hard cabin bench, I'll stand up to peer out the high forward windows, straining for the first sight of my island.

The prologue goes on to describe the island and its people, ending with these words: "But there were only the two of us, my sister, Caroline, and me, and neither of us could stay." The reader may assume that the body of the novel will explain why the narrator and her sister couldn't stay. In other words, the novel will backtrack from the prologue.

The prologue for the Newbery Honor book *The True Confessions of Charlotte Doyle*, by Avi, is titled "An Important Warning."

> Not every thirteen-year-old girl is accused of murder, brought to trial, and found guilty. But I was just such a girl, and my story is worth relating even if it did happen years ago. . . .

A second type of prologue is set in the past, before the events of the novel take place, and is usually set in the early youth of the protagonist. The purpose of this kind of prologue is to explain some trait, perhaps fear or hatred, that will play an important part in the story. In this prologue, the main story has not yet taken place, and there is not an omniscient POV. I selected this type of prologue for *Song of the Buffalo Boy*, set in 1989 in Vietnam. The prologue first takes place in 1973, when the protagonist is a little girl and the Americans pull out of Vietnam, and then in 1975, when South Vietnam falls to the Communists and thousands of refugees flee.

> The little girl is sitting in the middle of a room on a hard, sticky floor, watching the American soldier. His blue eyes twinkle and his white teeth gleam as he picks her up. She feels herself going high, higher than his smiling face, higher than his curly hair, so high that she must catch her breath. She feels lighthearted, like a bird in the top of a tamarind tree rocking with the wind. Above her head a dusty, squeaky ceiling fan slowly whirls, stirring her brown

hair, but she isn't afraid. The American soldier's big, strong hands have never dropped her before.

The prologue sets up the motivation behind the main goal of the protagonist—to find out who her American father is and to gain a sense of belonging.

The one risk with prologues is that many students and adults do not consider them as part of the story. They think of prologues as a kind of foreword or author's note—something to be skipped. So when you use a prologue, be aware that there will always be readers who will pass it by.

USE A FOREWORD OR AUTHOR'S NOTE FOR EXPLANATIONS

Unlike a prologue, which is part of the story and written as fiction, the *foreword* is nonfiction, and is usually a brief explanation of either how the story came about or some aspect of the story itself. Forewords are also referred to as *author's notes*. For historical novels, they often provide background material about the time period or people. The author's note for *Indio* starts like this:

> Along the banks of the Rio Grande, in the mountainous desert country of far west Texas, dwelled a peaceful farming people. They lived in square, flat-topped adobe houses and eked out a living by growing maize, beans and squash in limited areas near the river. . . .

Since the story itself does not depend on the foreword, many young adult readers avoid it altogether. But if it is brief and interestingly written, the foreword or author's note should be thought of as an added bonus for the reader. It may even mention reference books for further reading.

After your opening has hooked the reader, your next challenge is how to keep the reader turning the pages for the rest of the novel. This means creating characters the reader can identify with and characters they can love and care about.

Chapter Twelve

Creating Believable Characters

You probably have read a review of a novel that lamented cardboard, stereotyped or one-dimensional characters. These are the characters who do not come alive on the page, are so dull that the reader does not care about the characters' problems or fates, and are so flat that the reader does not remember the characters' names or anything about them after the book is closed.

At the opposite end of the spectrum are characters portrayed so vividly that you wouldn't be surprised to find them waiting on your doorstep one afternoon. These characters are so strong that you can close your eyes and see, hear and smell them. You understand them so well that you know what they would do or say in a given situation. Sherlock Holmes? Certainly. Huckleberry Finn? Of course. Scarlett O'Hara? Absolutely.

If, as a writer, you know your characters well enough, you can drop them into the plot and watch the story grow and develop practically on its own. It is a truly wonderful feeling when you can sit at the keyboard and feel that all you are doing is recording events taking place in front of your eyes as the characters live out their dramas and comedies, their hopes and dreams, their failures and triumphs.

The techniques used for developing characters for YA novels are the same as those used for adult novels, the only difference being the age of the protagonist. As with adult novels, before you begin to write your story, you should have specific characters in mind. Avoid trying to create the typical teen, or typical anyone for that matter. "Typical" leads to stereotyping. If the plot calls for a cheerleader, rather than creating the stereotypical pretty but snotty blonde, make her a sweet, freckled brunette who sleeps with a retainer in her mouth every night. If you need a librarian, don't automatically go for a woman with glasses, sensible shoes and fingers on the lips. Try a male dressed in a sweater, tie and blue jeans.

Avoid making characters too similar—similar names, appearance, speech patterns or personalities. The reader should be able to identify who has spoken without the necessary use of clarifying tags such as "Bill said," or "Mary said." In the real world, like snowflakes, no two people are exactly alike. It is the differences among us all that makes life interesting.

Characters come from the same places that ideas do—everywhere. Often you draw from someone you knew as a teen, a relative, a neighbor or someone you read about or saw on TV. But don't try to imitate a real person completely; that only leads to stiff, unbelievable characters. The best characters are those who combine the traits of many people you have met over the years; and every character will have a little bit of you in them. Once you decide who will play out the comedy or drama of your plot, the next step is to meet them.

GET TO KNOW YOUR MAIN CHARACTERS

You should know the characters' physical attributes, their past histories, families, likes and dislikes, fears, attitudes and beliefs. Once you have a thorough idea of who these people are, then it will be your job to convey these character traits to the reader by means of action and reaction, dialogue, internal thought and description. Some authors make extensive character biographies several pages long, while others keep only a few notes.

Physical Attributes

These include the obvious ones such as hair and eye color, skin tone, height, weight, body build, nose size and attractiveness to others. But physical attributes also include things such as speech patterns, voice tone and body language. How does the heroine walk—with a bold stride or as tense as a coiled rattlesnake? Does she laugh delicately or robustly from her belly? Does the protagonist always clear his throat before telling a lie, or swallow hard when he's scared? Once a character has been described, reiterate physical traits occasionally to remind the reader what the character looks like. This does not mean you must refer to your hero's blue eyes on every other page, but if he is short, he may need to stand on a stool to reach the upper shelf.

Family History

Unless the protagonist is a foundling, you should not only know where and when he was born, but also who his parents, grandparents and sometimes even his great-grandparents were. How many brothers and sisters does he have, and what was his rank in the family? Was he a wise older child, a carefree youngest child or a spoiled only child? Does he hate his sister or is he jealous of his brother? Did a twin die at birth? Is he an orphan? Are his parents divorced? Was he raised by a single parent? Is his family poor, middle class or filthy rich? Are his parents farmers, teachers, volunteers in the Peace Corps, immigrants, refugees or former slaves? Does he love visiting his crazy Aunt Petunia in Missouri during the summer? Because the protagonists of most young adult books are living at home, or at least are in contact with relatives, knowing the family environment is crucial to the story.

Experiences

Even siblings raised like peas in a pod will have different experiences. What happened to the hero when he was a baby? A toddler? In grade school? Did a playground bully push the hero into the water fountain and break his tooth? Did the hero almost drown in a swimming pool when he was five? Did a dog chase the heroine down the street every day after school when she was in the fourth grade? Did an older sister smack the hero when she caught him smoking behind the barn? Everything that happened to the protagonist will come together to help form his personality, memories and view of the world. If the heroine was sexually abused, she may grow up hating men. If the boy was locked in the closet as a child, he may grow up claustrophobic. Characters need to have a history and memories to rely on throughout the story. What happened to them in the past will influence their reactions and decisions.

Likes, Dislikes and Fears

What kind of food, clothes, animals, sports and places does the character like or dislike? Does he love the wind in his hair or the smell of rain in the air? Does she love the outdoors and hiking, or does she prefer to read a book in her room or go to the mall with her friends? Does he fear snakes or hate dogs? Does she like to wear black leather or cashmere? What are their hobbies or after school and weekend activities?

Many likes, dislikes and fears are tied to personal experiences. Sometimes a like, dislike or fear can be so strong that it becomes part of the plot. For example, in *Cabin 102* the protagonist is afraid of water because he almost drowned in a swimming pool when he was five. This fear plays a primary role in the way he acts and it causes him to get into one scrape after another.

Attitudes, Morals and Beliefs

What does the character believe in? Is he religious or not? Does he believe it is wrong to steal, kill or lie? How were these morals and beliefs instilled in him? Was he raised strictly? If writing about a non-American culture, the religion will often not be Judeo-Christian. The author must not pass judgment on the beliefs and moral values of other cultures. Some cultures allow a man to have several wives; a few cultures allow a woman to have several husbands; and some cultures of the past encouraged siblings or cousins to marry. Other cultures practice cannibalism. Does the hero believe in himself, or is he a rebel without a cause? Does he love his country, or does he burn the American flag? Is he superstitious or a devil-may-care free spirit who walks under ladders and wears the number thirteen on his jersey?

Personality

Everything else about a person can more or less be lumped into that generic term *personality*. Though personality is influenced by environment, babies are born with certain innate tendencies. Some cry a lot, others sleep a lot and still others coo and smile a lot. Is your protagonist shy or outgoing? Jovial or melancholy? A chatterbox or taciturn? A big flirt or terrified of the opposite sex?

DEVELOP A STRONG SUPPORTING CAST

Secondary characters are like supporting actors and actresses in the movies. They are not a main character, but the main characters' stories could not take place without them. They should be well-developed, but usually in less space and with less detail. For example, we may know several favorite foods of the protagonist, but only one or two of the secondary character. We may know the protagonist's family thoroughly, back three generations, but for the secondary character we may know only about his siblings.

The secondary character is often used to highlight the traits of the main character. This means that the secondary character might be the opposite of the protagonist. If the heroine is shy, an outgoing secondary emphasizes that trait. If she is short, make her best friend tall. In *Cabin 102*, the hero, Dusty, is terrified of drowning and avoids bodies of water. Tahni, the Arawak Indian girl, loves water, worships it and swims as free and uninhibited as a dolphin.

Although the secondary characters should be interesting, be careful not to let them run away with the story. If the little ham keeps demanding more lines and scenes, just promise her the starring role in a future book. Cut any runaway scenes and save them for your next novel.

Minor characters play even smaller roles than the primary and secondary characters. For this reason, little background material about them needs to be revealed. In a 45,000-word YA novel, there is simply not enough room to elaborate on intimate details of every character mentioned. A minor character may be a teacher, neighbor or sibling who does not appear in the story very often. Develop these characters only enough to play the part intended for them. In other words, if the math teacher only appears in one scene to give the students a test, a few lines of physical description or personality are enough.

Once you have gotten to know your characters, you will realize that they are more than just a physical description and a few "tags" such as twitching lips or a limp. Although most of the background material you have created will not be included in the story, knowing something about the characters before you begin will help you decide how they will speak, act and think. And as you write, the characters will reveal themselves to you even more. Sometimes you will discover that your initial ideas were wrong—the hero's aunt doesn't live on a farm in Missouri after all; she lives in a brownstone in Brooklyn. Don't be reluctant to change the character traits if you find that they are not working with the plot. Character and plot are intermingled, and each influences the other.

NAME YOUR CHARACTERS CAREFULLY

Part of the process of developing characters is giving them appropriate names, a task which can be as much fun or as frustrating as naming your own baby. Here are a few tips to keep in mind.

Names Reflect the Time Period. Some names have been around since the days of Chaucer, others were invented after World War II. Nothing frustrates me more than to see a modern name in a historical novel. The truth is, during early time periods in America, only a limited number of names were available. If you've ever done genealogy research, you know what I mean. Many times I have given thanks to a mother in the 1800s for having the audacity to name her son something other than John, William, James or George, or her daughter something other than Nancy, Sarah, Mary or Elizabeth. Whether your YA novel is set in contemporary times or the seventeenth century, make sure the first name was, or is, used in the novel's locale.

Sources for Names. When I write historical novels set in the United States, I like to use the names of my own ancestors. I'm sure they don't mind, and that way I can be sure the names are historically correct. For example, in *The Last Rainmaker*, I gave the heroine's father my great-great-grandfather's name, Andrew Jackson Long. (The heroine's name, Caroline Long, was one I saw in an 1870 census.) For my book in the Dear America series, I chose my great-grandmother's name, Lucinda Lawrence. Besides the census, you can also find interesting first names in period newspapers and magazines.

For first names from the 1920s to the present, go to the oldest high school in town and look through old yearbooks. Obituaries are good, too, but remember that if the person who died is elderly, the first name may no longer be popular. Baby name books list not only older names, but contemporary ones as well. And, of course, the birth announcements in the local newspaper will list current names. The telephone book is also wonderful for interesting first names and surnames, but avoid using a living person's entire name. If you do use someone's real name, you are advised to put a disclaimer in the front of the book explaining that "All characters in this book are fictitious and any resemblance to persons living or dead is purely coincidental."

Different ethnic groups have preferences for different names, as do certain regions of the United States and the world. In the 1940s and 1950s, it was common for southern children to have two first names, as do my sister Jackie Sue, my brother Jimmy Earl and my cousin Sherry Nell. Today this is not as common and may even be considered stereotyping. For interesting Spanish names I go to the telephone book, look up a popular surname and then look for appealing first names. I try to avoid the very common names like Maria and Juan, for this subtly hints of stereotyping. And for Vietnamese names, I use a Vietnamese telephone directory. However, I always verify my choices with someone from the culture to make sure that the name represents the gender I need, and does not translate into an unusual meaning. I learned this lesson the hard way. Once I selected a Chinese name for a YA novel. Later, after the book was already published, a Chinese friend informed me laughingly that the word I had chosen for the girl's name meant "fat."

One final note about names: Avoid giving different characters names that sound similar or start with the same letter, with the possible exception for twins or for humorous purposes. And don't bother to name very minor characters, unless it is to make a point or for humor; for example, a dentist named Dr. Payne.

GIVE YOUR PROTAGONIST GOALS

A crucial element in plot development is the goal of the character. Without a character goal, the story becomes no more than a string of events. The goal may be physical, such as learning to walk after an accident or learning to ride a horse after a bad fall. Survival stories often include physical goals such as climbing a mountain, crossing a river, riding out a storm or finding the way back home. The goal may be internalized, such as overcoming shyness, conquering grief or finding acceptance. A popular goal of YA novels is finding one's identity, whether by locating unknown relatives or by better understanding one's heritage. In mysteries, the primary goal is to solve the crime. In fantasies, the goal is often to save a kingdom. In a romance, the heroine's goal is to find true love.

All major characters will have goals and each character is not limited to just one. He may have several goals, some small and some grand. For example, the mystery hero may want to solve the crime, but also find out who his father was or overcome his fear of snakes. And sometimes, conflict will result from a clash of goals.

MAKE YOUR CHARACTERS GROW

As I read over my notes for this chapter, I came across a note-card that said "Characters should be consistent," then soon another one stating "Characters must change and grow." Now isn't that a contradiction? Actually, no.

Consistency refers to character traits and tags used throughout the story. For example, a tall character cannot suddenly be described as too short to reach the cabinet door in a later scene. Blue eyes should not suddenly become brown. A girl should not be a giggler in one scene and a wild cackler in another (unless she turns into a witch). A 90-pound weakling on page 3 better not, on page 103, be a big ox who can lift a 300-pound boulder, at least not without several paragraphs describing workouts and vitamins. A stutterer should not miraculously become stutter-free just for the convenience of a scene. I knew a writer who, in the final chapter of her unpublished pirate novel, had the heroine pick up a sword and defeat a blackheart in a thrilling duel. The only reference to the heroine's unusual skill came as she picked up the sword and said something like, "My father was a master swordsman and taught me everything he knew." The maiden's talent should have been mentioned several times before the duel, so that the last scene would have been believable. This is what is meant by consistency.

Change and growth refer not necessarily to physical traits, but to an internal metamorphosis of the protagonist. Growth implies learning something about life, people or oneself. It may be related to a physical change, but it is more than that. For example, in *Cabin 102*, Dusty, who is terrified of drowning, undergoes a gradual emotional change after befriending the ghost of an Arawak Indian girl who loves water. In the end of the book, a tidal wave knocks several cruise passengers overboard. After a frightening night alone in the ocean, Dusty not only overcomes his fear of water, but also realizes the importance of his family. As a result, he goes on to communicate with his father for the first time since his parents' divorce.

Growth of a character is often the main purpose of a story. It is the heart of the theme, a universal truth. Growth should be a gradual and natural outcome from events in the story; it should be the logical conclusion. If Dusty had gone through all the events of the book and still hated his father and feared the water, what would have been the story's point in the first place?

MAKE THE PROTAGONIST LIKABLE

Adult readers may force themselves to wade through a great work of literature despite the fact that they hate the hero or heroine. But young readers will toss the book aside if they don't like or identify with the main character. To create a character that no adolescent can resist, remember these strategies.

Avoid perfection. Protagonists do not need to be perfect, either physically or mentally; in fact, a few flaws make them more human. The imperfection may come from physical appearance, personality flaws or from home life. They may be flunking math or may be clumsy.

Hand out some problems. If the hero had no problems, there would be no story. The problem is often an obstacle that prevents the hero from achieving his goal and thus causes conflict. (Conflict is discussed in chapter fourteen.) And usually the problems are many; as soon as he solves one, another pops up. The main problem should be important to not only the hero but also to the reader. If the only problem the protagonist has is what clothes to wear to school, who will care?

Make the characters struggle. The protagonist must struggle to solve or overcome a problem. The larger the problem and the greater the struggle, the more heroic the character will become. The hero is not one who stands on the sidelines and watches or wrings his hands. The likable hero is one who jumps in and participates in the action, who does something to attain his goal and to overcome a problem. He does not always succeed, but his courage and determination make him admirable.

Let characters attain wisdom. As previously mentioned, the hero will change and grow. He will gain wisdom from his struggle. If the hero were to end up the same way he started, how could the reader admire him?

DON'T OVERWRITE THE VILLAIN

Think back to villains you have met in literature over the years. The ones you probably remember the most are the ones that have some admirable traits along with the bad. You may have even liked the villain more than the hero at times.

A villain should be multidimensional and not totally evil. Unless you are describing a space creature or monster, a villain will be human, with human desires and foibles. For example, a bully who beats up the hero and steals his lunch money in one scene, may rescue a homeless dog in another.

A villain will have goals, some good and some bad, but his major goal should be in opposition to the hero's goals, and thus creates conflict. The more intelligent, crafty and admirable the villain is, the more we admire the hero in the end when he declares victory.

In *Shadow of the Dragon*, one villain is a skinhead named Frank Schultz. Although he belongs to a racist gang and participates in acts of violence, because he is the brother of the hero's girlfriend, the reader discovers many things about Frank's background that explain why he acts as he does.

MAKE YOUR CHARACTERS COME ALIVE

Once you have created the characters and have a good sense of who they are and what they want, the next task is to convey this information to the reader. There are three basic tools used to develop a character: description, action and reaction, and dialogue. To avoid repetition, let's consider the first two tools now and save dialogue—which is, to many writers, the most important tool—for chapter thirteen.

Description. Young readers like to know what the protagonist looks like. They want to know about any unique physical features and any unusual clothing or hairstyles. Sometimes they will look at the dust jacket and use the picture as a model for the protagonist. That is one reason why a good cover can increase the sales of YA novels. However, because few authors have control over what the covers of their books will look like, narrative description is the most simple and reliable way to convey a character's physical appearance. This was the common method used by authors in the past, and page after page of description and background material was often used each time a new character was introduced. This is no longer a popular method. Today's readers are more action-oriented and do not appreciate long descriptive passages. Description should be broken into shorter sections and combined with dialogue and action.

For example, in *Song of the Buffalo Boy*, I wanted the reader to know that Loi, the seventeen-year-old Amerasian girl, was tall. Instead of using a lengthy paragraph of description, I revealed her height in snippets of information interwoven with thought and action:

> . . . [Loi] sat up and stretched, brushing her fingertips against the hair of her youngest cousin, who lay asleep on the cot next to hers. How long had her arms been able to reach that far, she wondered. It seemed like only a year ago that her body fit neatly inside the confines of the thin straw mattress. Now her feet were hanging over the edge of her low cot.

Action and reaction. The second way to develop a character is through the character's actions. Imagine a group of teenagers waiting in a cafeteria line. Each person in line is a unique human being with a distinct personality. This is revealed through each teenager's actions. What would happen if a big hulk of a boy, Billy, cut in line and elbowed his way to the front? Would all of the teens in line react the same way? No, of course not. An aggressive person might shout and shove back, while a timid person might stare at the floor and say nothing. A cowardly person might throw something and then quickly duck and hide. The class clown might make faces and gestures, while a goody-two-shoes might report the incident to the teacher. A whiner might complain but do nothing, while the heroic person boldly confronts the bully and asks him to move to the back of the line.

In real life, people do totally illogical things; but in fiction, consistency of action is important when developing a character. If the hero acts bold on one page, shy on another page and funny on yet another, the reader will receive mixed signals and not be able to get a solid picture of the character. If a hero does act differently, there should be a good reason and an explanation.

Reaction is similar to action, but it usually refers to the way others react in relation to the hero, rather than the way the hero acts himself. Using our cafeteria-line example, if the protagonist in the story is Billy, the teen who cut in line, his actions seem to reveal that he is aggressive, thoughtless and a bully. The reactions of the other characters will reveal what they think of him, and thus help to develop his character. For example, let's say that everyone in the line sports a look of shock, and someone whispers, "What's gotten into Billy? Why, I've never seen him cut in line before"; "Something must be wrong with Billy. He's usually at the end of the line"; or "Oh, don't bother with Billy. He's big, but he's harmless. They say his mother dropped him on his head when he was a baby." As you can see, the reactions of the other students have given Billy a whole new personality.

One of the great pleasures of writing is breathing life into a flat, cardboard entity lying on the page (or computer screen) in front of you. You, the author, must be able to become the characters you are writing about. You must become the rice farmer in Vietnam, the Indian girl captured by Spaniards or the boy drifting down the river on a raft. You must know your characters so well that you can predict how they will act and think in any given situation. You must also know how they will speak because, as chapter thirteen shows, dialogue is one of the most important aspects of any YA novel.

Putting Words in Your Characters' Mouths

Pick up any young adult paperback novel and you will notice an abundance of dialogue. In fact, some YA series seem to be mostly dialogue. Before choosing a novel to read, many young readers flip through the pages looking for lots of white space and short paragraphs, two things created by the use of dialogue. Young readers love dialogue for several reasons: They are accustomed to watching TV and movies, which rely heavily on dialogue; it can be read faster than narrative and is usually more entertaining to read. When characters are speaking, everyone tends to sit up and listen. For all of these reasons, good dialogue can make or break a story.

Dialogue is one of the most powerful tools authors have at their command. But before you can use this tool, you must understand what dialogue is and how it works.

DIALOGUE VS. CONVERSATION

Many novice writers make the mistake of assuming that anything placed in quotation marks is acceptable dialogue. If it were that easy, we would all be best-selling authors. I once critiqued a manuscript in which the characters carried on a long, boring conversation that included talk about relatives' health, groceries and the dog's trip to the vet. None of the spoken material was relevant to the story, and it did not move the plot forward. When I mentioned this to the writer, she quickly said, "Oh, but this is a real conversation that I overheard between my two aunts." And she was correct. It was indeed a conversation. But conversation is not dialogue. Eavesdrop on a group of teens and you will hear them interrupting each other, talking at the same time, cursing, laughing, using incomplete sentences and incorrect grammar, going off on tangents, changing the subject and some-times talking with their mouths full. That is real life. That is real conversation. And if your novel used that sort of material, the reader would throw it down in frustration.

EFFECTIVE WAYS TO USE DIALOGUE

Dialogue is just as important as narrative, description and plot. It is not haphazard. To the contrary, dialogue is usually well thought out and serves a purpose. Here are the major ways authors use dialogue as a tool.

To develop character. What a person says is an inherent part of that person's character. To give a very elementary example, suppose a group of teens are standing on the sidewalk when a leather bag filled with money falls out of a passing truck. An honest-Abe character would say something like "Let's take it to the police station down the street. You know we don't have the right to keep it," while a greedy character would announce "Finder's keepers. If I get it first, you can eat my dust." A para-noid character might remark "Don't touch it. It's probably a bomb in disguise," and an existential character might say "It's only money; it can't buy happiness."

Dialogue has the ability to reveal aspects of the character's background and personality. Dialogue containing incorrect grammar, short words and the use of the word *ain't* implies someone with lesser education than dialogue that uses complex sentences and flowery language. Dialogue can reveal the birth-place of the character. For example, the character may speak with an Irish brogue or a Southern accent. Dialogue can also reveal the age of the character: Compare *swell* to *groovy* or *awesome*.

To reveal background. Besides character development, dia-logue may replace a lengthy flashback or a long narrative to relay background information. This is important in YA and middle-grade novels where word space is at a premium. In *Indio*, I could have used numerous paragraphs to explain that a drought was upon the land and that the pueblo dwellers had done everything within their power to bring about rain. Instead, I chose a brief dialogue between the heroine, Ipa-tah-chi, and her older brother, Ximi. Here, Ipa-tah-chi is explaining why she is on top of a cliff overlooking a river just before dawn.

"I thought if we saw the panther, we could pray to its spirit for rain."

"Pray for rain?" Ximi laughed. "You, a little girl of [ten summers]. . . . Ha! You would pray to the Panther Spirit and bring rain when our pueblo elders have been singing and dancing for more days than hairs on Little Brother's head? Ha!"

To foreshadow. Foreshadowing is the delicate art of hinting at the future without giving it away. Dialogue is often more subtle than narrative, since the character speaking may not know that he is predicting the future.

In *Indio*, Ipa-tah-chi says of her younger brother, Kadoh, ". . . I should not have brought him. He is afraid of the dark." Kadoh's fear of the dark will play an important role in the future, when he is forced by Spaniards to work underground in a silver mine. At the end of the novel, when Kadoh begins to crack under the pressure, the reader should not be surprised because the fear had been foreshadowed.

To convey setting. As shown in previous examples, dialogue is a shortcut that eliminates the need for long passages of description. Personally, I love description, but many of today's readers do not. So instead of writing three paragraphs describing the setting, you might have the heroine of a novel proclaim: "Oh, Sam, look at the mountains. I never dreamed they would be so breathtaking. And the smell! It's like a Christmas tree lot."

Dialogue can also create the flavor of a setting. For example, if a story is set in a foreign land, a sprinkling of foreign language in the dialogue helps to establish the locale. The same holds true for stories set in certain regions of the United States. It is important, however, not to use too much dialect or too many foreign words, for that will slow the reader down and interfere with the pacing. Just a hint here and there is all that is needed.

To describe characters. Dialogue is a fast way to convey physical descriptions of the characters. In *Song of the Buffalo Boy*, the protagonist is a seventeen-year-old Amerasian girl. Her response to a compliment from a young man illustrates to the reader what she looks like:

"Why do you call me beautiful, when all the other villagers call me ugly and *con-hoang*—fatherless child? See, my hair is not as thick and straight as yours, and my eyes do not have the beautiful slant of yours. And my skin—how I detest these freckles on my nose! I want to look like you and your family. I hate being different."

To relay information and develop plot. Sometimes it is more prudent and time-saving to have a character say what is happening. For example, in the following scene from *Indio*, the Indians have learned that strangers (Spaniards) are on their way to the village. The elders hold council while the women and children wait in the adobe houses. Ipa-tah-chi's aunt awakens her while it is still dark.

> "What is wrong?" Ipa asked as she rubbed her eyes.
> "The council has made the decision. The women and children will go to the mountains to hide from the strangers."
> Ipa sat up and watched her aunt flutter about the room gathering her best pots and deerskins. She placed them in the middle of the floor.
> "Auntie, what are you doing?" Ipa asked as an uneasy feeling crept over her.
> "The council decided that we must offer gifts to the strangers so they will leave us in peace. A messenger from the lower village arrived last night. He told us that the strangers will take what they want anyway, so it is better to appease them early. Fetch those fancy baskets that I have been saving for your wedding day and put them in this pile."

This dialogue reveals to the reader that the Spaniards are almost to the village, the women and children will flee, there is the strong possibility of a pillage and the villagers are peaceful and want to avoid a fight.

One thing writers should avoid, however, is dialogue that is too full of information and facts. Such dialogue will come across as stilted and unnatural. Here's an example:

> "Frank, I'd like you to meet my Uncle George. He was born in 1898 and fought in World War I in France, then married my Aunt Sally in 1925 and raised seven children on a pig farm before discovering oil in the backyard and

becoming overnight millionaires who moved to California and own a house in Malibu and Hollywood and a log cabin in Aspen."

To make transitions. The purpose of transition is to change scenes or chapters with as little disruption to the reader as possible. Dialogue is an easy way to make the transition smooth and seamless. Imagine that our fourteen-year-old protagonist, Henry, ended a scene with: "I've got to find that missing pendant or my sister will skin me alive."

The next scene opens with his baseball buddy running up to Henry's front porch, exclaiming

> "Henry! Where have you been all day? I've been calling you since nine o'clock. I was afraid you'd miss tonight's game."
>
> "I was looking for that stupid pendant I lost." Henry glanced over his shoulder to make sure his sister wasn't within earshot. "I couldn't find it. Guess I'll have to buy another one."

With only a few sentences, the reader has been transported to the end of the day and knows, without hearing all the little details, that Henry had a frustrating and unsuccessful search. When condensing time in this manner, keep in mind that scenes within one chapter typically do not cover long periods of time. Passages of longer periods of time are usually saved for the beginning of a new chapter.

TIPS FOR WRITING GOOD DIALOGUE

It takes patience and practice to develop good dialogue. Read several YA novels and compare the dialogue. Did you find that sometimes it seemed to flow as smooth as honey, while other times it was awkward, stilted or unbelievable? When you find a book with great dialogue, read more work by the author. Read passages aloud until you get a feel for the sound of good dialogue. While writing your own stories, read your dialogue out loud, too, or have a friend read it to you. Do you stumble over certain words or phrases? Does it seem silly or melodramatic?

Here are a few other tips to keep in mind:

1. Make sure the reader knows who is speaking without relying

heavily on identifying tags such as "so-and-so said"; do this by giving each character a distinct voice. Boys speak differently than girls. Foreigners have accents. Regions have dialects. Speech patterns differ from person to person.

2. Avoid excessive slang. Today's cute phrases will be cold and outdated within a few years—maybe even by the time your novel is published.

3. Cut out the undesirable aspects of an actual conversation, such as throat-clearing, interrupting one another, losing the train of thought, changing subject matter midsentence, uhs, ahs, hmms and mispronunciations.

4. Do not ramble, even though people often do so in real life. Dialogue must serve a purpose and move the story forward.

5. Do not interject too much description or narrative between dialogue. This causes the reader to lose the flow of the dialogue and destroys its impact.

6. Use only "speaking" verbs such as *said, spoke, replied, shouted, called out, screamed, whispered* or *cried.* Here are a few common examples of verbs used incorrectly.

   "That's so funny," she laughed.
   (You cannot *laugh* words.)
   "That's so gruesome," she grimaced.
   (You cannot *grimace* words.)
   "That's so disgusting," she frowned.
   (You cannot *frown* words.)
   "That's so sad," she sighed.
   (You cannot *sigh* words.)
   "That's so exciting!" she panted.
   (You cannot *pant* words.)

The correct way to express the above dialogue would be: "That's so funny," she said, laughing; or "That's so funny," she said with a laugh; or "That's so sad," she said and sighed; or "That's so sad." She sighed.

PROFANITY

There was a time when words like *hell* or *damn* were not allowed in novels for adults, much less those for adolescents. But within the past few years, more and more profanity has appeared in an emerging category called *realistic* YA literature. These novels are often defined by such adjectives as *hard-hitting* or *gutsy,* and deal with issues that reflect the problems of today's adolescents—gang violence, sex, drugs, abuse and incest. Not only are the stories realistic, but the language is, too. A novel about soldiers in the Vietnam War, for instance, naturally has a few cuss words. A story dealing with an angry, abusive father might use even stronger language. Certain editors seek out these types of novels and allow the author to use whatever profanity they feel the story requires.

I have worked with teenagers, mostly boys ages twelve to fourteen (some of whom were gang members), and I know from firsthand experience how very strong their language can be. Nevertheless, I choose not to use profanity in my YA novels. Many authors would say that I am being unrealistic, but it is my philosophy that the readers already know profanity and do not need to see it spelled out. If a scene calls for strong language, I simply say something like "Henry spewed out a stream of profanity that would curl the toes of any sailor," or "My ears are still burning from what Papa said next." Without actually using the words, the interpretation is still the same.

Each author must use his or her own judgment. Editors will let you know if they feel the profanity is gratuitous. Keep in mind, however, that the more profanity your YA novel contains, the more it will be banned by schools. You have to weigh the consequences: Would you prefer to have a profanity-free book that will be read by many students, or a book with more realistic language that will be read by fewer young adults?

Whether your dialogue is squeaky clean or blistering hot, it must captivate the readers and transport them into the scene. It must also be an integral part of the plot. In other words, it should move the story forward, not slow it down.

Chapter Fourteen

The Bumpy Road of Plot

W hat keeps the reader turning the pages? Plot. Simply put, *plot* is a matter of cause and effect: what happens to the characters and how they react. Plot is what holds the story together, the center around which the characters, dialogue and setting revolve. Without plot, you do not have a story. For many authors, plot is the most difficult part of writing. But once you analyze its individual components, developing a plot becomes a monster that anyone can conquer.

Think of plot as a long ribbon of highway down which the reader will travel. Which is more interesting, a road that is flat and straight as far as the eye can see, or one that curves, goes around scary bends, over mountains and down valleys? If you want to captivate your readers, take them on the latter road, giving them a plot full of highs and lows, victories and defeats, surprises and suspense.

Many reference books have been written to explain plot: *Thirty-Six Dramatic Situations* by Georges Polti, *20 Master Plots* by Ronald B. Tobias and *How to Write Plots That Sell* by F.A. Rockwell. These authors agree that there is a set number of plot possibilities and that all stories will follow the pattern of one of these possibilities. For YA novels, among the most common plots are the journey (quest), adventure, romance, survival, coming of age, underdog and whodunit.

But no matter what the plot, it relies on this simple formula: character + goal + obstacles + resolution. Character is discussed in chapter twelve. Now let's look at the remaining elements of the formula and at devices for developing plot.

GIVE YOUR PROTAGONIST GOALS

Every protagonist must have a goal, and it must be vital. It should be worthy and it must be important to the hero or heroine. *Important* does not necessarily mean life-threatening, and, of course, the goal varies depending on the age of the protagonist. For example, a seven-year-old hero may have the goal of outsmarting a neighborhood bully, while a seventeen-year-old may have the goal of attending an Ivy League college or finding a summer job.

Goals should be realistic and believable. For example, a twelve-year-old boy should not have the goal of obtaining a driver's license. That is a *dream*. However, he can have the goal of convincing his older brother to let him drive the car on a country road. One of the differences between paperback series fiction and hardback literature lies in the goals of the characters. In a mystery, the goal will be to solve the crime; in a romance, to get the boy or girl; and in a survival story, simply to stay alive.

CONFLICT—THROW OBSTACLES IN THE PATH

Once you have established the main goal for the hero, you must throw obstacles in his path so that he cannot easily achieve that goal. This is often referred to as *conflict*. Call it torture or sadism, but you, with your god-like power, must subject the hero or heroine to storms, fires, vicious animals, broken hearts, abusive parents and fatal illnesses—to every conceivable kind of problem. These obstacles arise from five basic situations:

- Man vs. nature (disease, natural disasters, mountains, rivers)
- Man vs. man (hero vs. villain)
- Man vs. society (hero vs. rules, laws, religion)
- Man vs. internal fears (psychological obstacles)
- Man vs. unknown (supernatural, fantasy, science fiction)

When speaking to young authors, I use an analogy to which they all can relate—a video game. Even archaic ones such as Ms. PacMan rely on the same basic premise of obstacles and levels. The first level is challenging but fairly easy. The hero fights off some falling boulders, a fire-breathing dragon or an evil kung-fu master. As each obstacle is overcome, another is presented until that level is completed. The obstacles of the second level are more difficult, the difficulty increasing with each level until the hero finally rescues the princess. Now I admit that video games are not literature, but presenting obstacles that become more and more difficult is the foundation for a good plot.

When the protagonist faces the obstacle, a *crisis* occurs. Returning to the twelve-year-old who wants to drive the car: Suppose he talks his older brother into letting him take the wheel when they reach a deserted country road. He has achieved his first goal—getting to drive. Now suppose he is merrily going along, swerves to miss a rabbit, loses control of the car and runs into a ditch. The tires blow out and the motor won't start. Here is crisis number one. Next, suppose his brother collapses with a bleeding head wound. Here is crisis number two. The boy flags down a passing pickup and thankfully puts his brother in the back. The driver says he will send a tow truck for the car. The boy has solved crises one and two, but as they travel along he realizes the driver is an infamous escaped convict. Crisis number three has arrived.

Each problem becomes progressively more difficult, and as it is resolved, a new, even more challenging one arises. Sometimes the problem is not solved. The hero may try to escape, but fails. Or he may make a decision that he thinks will solve the problem, but in fact it makes matters worse. This is called *cause and effect*. He will have to constantly re-evaluate and reset his goals. These failures help to create *tension*. If the reader knows the hero is capable of failing, the emotions are stronger when danger presents itself again.

The obstacles and crises become progressively more dangerous or more complex, until the final obstacle seems to be insurmountable. But remember the old saying "It's always darkest before the dawn." Just when the reader thinks all is lost, the hero resolves the problem. And in children's and young adult novels, it is the protagonist who must save the day, not his parents, a *deus ex machina* (heavenly intervention), or the cavalry coming to the rescue. In other words, the hero must *struggle*. Without this struggle, the reader will feel cheated and that the hero got off easy. Such a hero will not earn the reader's respect.

CREATE TENSION AND SUSPENSE

All novels, whether a whodunit mystery or a love story, must have suspense. Suspense makes the reader curious to know what happens next and keep turning the pages to find out. The reader is worried about the hero or heroine, which is one reason why having a sympathetic protagonist is so important in YA fiction. Create suspense by not giving all the information at once, by raising questions in the reader's mind, and by making the reader wonder how the hero will get out of the jam.

BE AWARE OF PACING

Pacing is the rate at which the plot is revealed to the reader. It is one of the most difficult aspects of novel writing to grasp, and bad pacing has been the downfall of many authors. Has anyone ever told you that your story drags, seems jumpy or is confusing? All this can be repaired by working on your pacing, by balancing dialogue, narrative, exposition and action throughout the story.

Every work of fiction is composed of *scenes* and *sequels*. Scenes contain the action, the dialogue and emotion. In a scene something is happening; scenes are naturally faster paced and more exciting. Sequels contain the explanations, the descriptions and the narrative. In sequels, the protagonist is often steeped in internal thoughts, and no action is occurring. Sequels slow the pace.

The natural pace of writing involves a scene, followed by a sequel, followed by a scene, followed by a sequel and so on. A chapter may open with either one, but action novels often open with a scene. Scenes evoke emotions, while sequels let the reader's emotions rest. In both scenes and sequels, short sentences speed the pace and long sentences slow it.

A novel that has several back-to-back scenes leaves the reader breathless and worn out. A novel that has several sequels back to back leaves the reader bored and longing for action. Long passages of description slow the pace. Chapters with all dialogue feel shallow; chapters with no dialogue feel tedious.

When considering your pacing, be aware of *momentum*, the gradual progression of the story. As tension mounts, the action grows faster and the story moves forward. The pace moves faster toward the end of the story, especially in action novels.

Flashbacks tend to slow the momentum. For YA novels, much of the information contained in a flashback can, and should, be revealed through dialogue. If you use flashbacks, short is better than long, and any flashback, though it describes action that took place in the past, must add to the forward movement of the story.

After writing your rough draft, go through it and highlight dialogue, action, exposition and narrative with different colored markers. If one color dominates the others, you have a clue where to begin revising. Or use a colored pencil to mark each scene and sequel. Sometimes a simple rearrangement of material is all it takes to correct the pacing. And if you still have trouble with pacing, read as many good YA novels as you can. Read the types of books you are interested in writing. After a while you will begin to sense what works best.

PRACTICE SMOOTH TRANSITIONS

Transitions do not need to be long and complicated. Simpler is often better. Suppose your heroine is in a house and you want to get her to the nearby high school gymnasium for a basketball game. No need to describe how she got her keys, walked out the door, started the car, drove down Mulberry Lane, parked the car, entered the gym, got dressed in her uniform and so on. A far better transition would be: "After driving to the gymnasium, Mary suited up and waited for the Tigers to walk onto the court."

AVOID COINCIDENCES

Yes, coincidences do occur in real life. Many bizarre things have happened to me and to people I know. You can always tell when a made-for-TV movie is based on real events, because those are the movies that are full of coincidences and often irrational behavior. But relying on coincidence to move the plot forward is lazy writing and will make you lose the reader's respect. Oddly enough, fiction has to be more logical and believable than real life.

DOES IT END WITH A BANG OR A WHIMPER?

Endings in YA novels may be nail-biting tense or rose-petal sweet, but one thing they should not be is predictable. Predictability is boring. Maintain the suspense all the way to the end. This is especially crucial in mysteries; you do not want the reader to know who committed the crime until that final climactic scene. On the other hand, you must also be consistent. There should be no unfair surprises; for example, a distant cousin who was never mentioned turning out to be the murderer. To avoid those sudden surprises, use foreshadowing throughout the story.

A *climax* is the protagonist's response to a crisis. A typical novel has several small crises and climaxes throughout; every time the hero overcomes an obstacle or has a revelation, it is a miniclimax. The *ultimate climax* is the highest point in the story, where that last, seemingly insurmountable obstacle is wrestled and the hero emerges victorious or vanquished. If the hero is vanquished, the story becomes a tragedy.

After the climax comes the *dénouement,* a few pages of explanation that calms the reader and prepares him for the ending. In mysteries, this is where the detective explains the clues and ties everything together. In a romance, this is where the girl and boy explain their past behavior and vow their eternal love. In a coming-of-age book, this is where the protagonist matures and puts away childish things.

In YA novels not all endings are happy; however, they should be hopeful, and something should be resolved. The hero has grown, has learned something about his inner being, is a better person for what has transpired and has come to a new realization. Perhaps the village is destroyed by the volcano, but the hero will relocate and build again, and will carry on the traditions of his deceased parents. Perhaps the car is demolished, but the boy comes to realize that his relationship with his brother is more important than anything else. Perhaps someone has died, but his spirit will be remembered and his work carried on. Young adult readers love drama, and most are still optimists at heart, so give them an ending that they will remember for a lifetime.

Chapter Fifteen

The Power of the Written Word

I remember the first time I checked books out of the library. I spent many exciting hours poring over the words in those books, living the lives of many characters and sharing their joys and heartbreaks. I escaped to other worlds and, at least for a few hours, forgot my own woes. All this because of words strung together in a logical order, selected by an author to bring readers to the brink of ecstasy or plummet them to the depths of sadness.

It is often said that language is what separates humans from animals; that the ability to communicate, and written communication in particular, is the basis for all human achievement. Think about what the written word can do: It can cause wars and destroy nations, it can bring laugher or tears, it can change lives and it can save souls.

How does an author use words in the most powerful way? To begin with, you should have reliable references. The basic four are an updated dictionary, a thesaurus, a book of English grammar rules and a book of writing composition or style. Two standards in the latter category are *The Elements of Style* by Strunk and White, and *The Chicago Manual of Style*. (The list of references in the Appendix includes several others.) Keep these sources near your desk, and don't be afraid to use them, especially after the rough draft is finished and you are starting the revisions.

MASTER THE PARTS OF SPEECH

To play on that old Chinese adage, a novel of a thousand pages begins with a single word—words like nouns, verbs, adjectives and adverbs. How you select and use words will make your story weak or strong. Let's consider the various parts of speech.

Nouns and Pronouns

The first rule of noun selection is *be specific*. For example, rather than saying "The man walked down the street," be more precise and say "The postman walked down the street," or "The coal miner walked down the street." Always try to evoke the most exact and vivid image when selecting nouns.

Use variety. Avoid repeating the same noun twice in the same sentence, or several times in the same paragraph. Here is where a thesaurus can be helpful. For example, the word *postman* may be interchanged with *mailman, mail carrier* or *postal employee*. If your novel is set in a foreign country or in a subculture in America, an occasional foreign word substituted for a noun adds strength to the story; for example, a grocer in Little Italy might call the mailman *il postino*.

Avoid unclear pronouns. You may have read, and probably written, sentences such as: "Mary saw her walking down the street and she quickly turned away." Who turned away? Compare that to: "As she saw her Aunt Caroline walking down the street, Mary quickly turned away." The same rule applies to dialogue. The use of the basic "he said" or "she said" is often enough to clarify who is speaking. But sometimes, especially in a case where several speakers are of the same sex, you will need to use the speaker's name or a tag such as "the redhead said" or "the cowboy said."

Do not overuse proper names. This may seem like a contradiction of the last rule, but overusing proper names is a sign of lazy writing. This is especially true for dialogue, as demonstrated by the following example:

> "Hi, Thomas," said the postman. "I thought you were on vacation, Thomas."
> "I got sick and couldn't go."
> "That's too bad, Thomas. Here's your mail."
> "Thanks."
> "Well, Thomas, hope you get to feeling better."

Simple is usually best. Some authors claim that when given a choice between an Anglo-Saxon word and a Latin-based word, they choose the first. Anglo-Saxon words are a combination of the Old English and Germanic languages and are often shorter and harsher sounding. Latin-derived words are often combinations of several words and softer sounding. For example, the word cow comes from Old English; *bovine* come from Latin. In action scenes, shorter Anglo-Saxon words are often more emotionally charged than long Latin-derived words.

Verbs

The use of powerful verbs can make an ordinary story strong. Not surprisingly, the rules for verb selection are similar to those for noun selection.

Be precise. Again, use the thesaurus. Select verbs that evoke a strong sense of the location, character, mood and scene. Compare "Jack cut his victims" to "Jack lacerated his victims" to "Jack mutilated his victims." The verb you select will depend on whether it is part of a narrative or dialogue. A policeman on the beat would probably use *cut*, a doctor would use *lacerated*, and a newspaper article might use *mutilated*. The more specific the verb, the more likely it is to create a strong visual image. Compare "He walked across the room" to "He darted across the room" to "He sauntered across the room" to "He sneaked across the room" to "He skipped across the room."

Use variety. Again, avoid using the same verb several times in the same paragraph. But do not go to the opposite extreme and use uncommon or inappropriate verbs just to avoid repeating one.

Avoid passive tense. This is one of the most common mistakes I find when critiquing works of fiction. In passive tense, the subject of the sentence is being acted upon rather than doing the action. Compare these sentences:

> Henry was bitten by the dog.
> Sally was turned away at the front door.
> Joey was called up to the stage.

To remedy the passive tense, switch the subject and object, as in the following:

> The dog bit Henry.
> The butler turned Sally away at the front door.
> The director called Joey up to the stage.

When I taught a creative writing class, I asked students to bring different colored highlighter pens and to go through their rough drafts marking various parts of speech. The students were amazed at the number of passive verbs they had used.

Use simple past tense. Many writers confuse passive verbs, such as *was hit* or *was driven*, with verbs using the imperfect tense. For example, the sentence "Carrie *was running* as fast as she could" is not passive tense, but "Carrie *was run* off the road" is. Use simple past tense (e.g.,"Carrie *ran* as fast as she could") rather than imperfect tense, unless you want to express a continuing action (e.g., "Back then, Carrie *was running* every morning before breakfast").

Present tense is rarely used in YA fiction and requires skillful handling to be successful. When used, present tense often denotes a dream sequence, an internal monologue, dialogue or a first person narrative.

Adjectives

Adjectives modify nouns. They should be treated like spices added to a recipe: Too few and the food is bland; too many and they overwhelm the flavor of the dish.

Be frugal. Adjectives can be beautiful and moving, but a string of unnecessary adjectives destroys the power of the noun. Whenever possible, let the noun stand on its own (the more you use specific, concrete nouns, the easier this will be). Rarely is more than one adjective necessary. Compare "A tall, skinny, awkward boy walked into the room" to "A gangly boy walked into the room."

Don't be redundant. Some nouns by nature do not require adjectives. For example, saying *dark shadow* or *black shadow* is redundant—is a shadow ever light or white? How about *wet water, cold ice* or *hot fire*?

Evoke mood. The adjective should convey mood, emotion or action that matches the contents of the sentence. As an exercise, write down a common noun and then change its mood or meaning by adding different adjectives. Forest can become *dense forest, enchanted forest, inviting forest, forbidden forest, menacing forest, verdant forest* or *fragrant forest*. Each adjective creates a different picture. In this manner the most ordinary nouns can become vivid.

Adverbs

Adverbs modify verbs, adjectives and other adverbs. The rules for the use of adjectives apply to adverbs as well. Too many adverbs slow the narrative and interrupt the flow of the sentence.

One of the easiest ways to eliminate unnecessary adverbs is to select strong, descriptive verbs. Here are a few examples:

"The cowboy walked across the room boldly" becomes "The cowboy strode across the room"; "The cowboy walked across the room angrily" becomes "The cowboy stomped across the room"; and, "The cowboy walked across the room gingerly" becomes "The cowboy tiptoed across the room."

The same rules may also be applied to *prepositional phrases* that modify verbs. For example, "The cowboy walked across the room with determination" is less effective than "The cowboy marched across the room."

SHOW, DON'T TELL

This is one of the most basic rules of writing good fiction, and every writer will hear it mentioned many times. Yet many novice authors neglect this simple rule. *Tell* means you dictate to the reader what is or has happened. If you write "Julie was embarrassed that the little rabbit had scared her," you have told the reader that Julie was embarrassed. *Show* means you demonstrate, with dialogue or action, what has happened. The revised sentence might be "Julie drew in a deep breath and felt her face blush when she saw that only a little rabbit had made the noise." Or this version, using dialogue: "Julie drew in a deep breath. 'Why, it's just a little rabbit. How silly of me to be so scared.'"

You will notice that showing naturally takes more words than telling. Some telling is allowed, but it is better to save it for passages of narrative exposition.

AVOID CLICHÉS

A *cliché* is a word, a phrase or even an idea that has been used so many times that it has lost its originality. A few examples are: thick as pea soup, light as a feather, mad as a hatter, bad to the bone and crazy like a fox. Clichés are a sign of lazy writing, for it takes longer and requires more effort to create a new image. Yet new images have far greater power. Everyone has seen the phrase "as white as snow," but I once saw the phrase "as white as a baby's new tooth." That image startled me and, though I read it years ago, it remains vivid in my mind.

AVOID UNNECESSARY QUALIFIERS

Words like *too, just, even, next, maybe, almost* and *sort of* clutter up sentences without adding to their meaning. I have been guilty of using the word *just*, as in "I *just* wanted to kiss you," "I *just* wanted to say hello" and "He is *just* ten years old." Delete the word *just* from each of those sentences and the meaning has not changed at all; in fact, it becomes clearer.

USE POETIC DEVICES

Too many authors mistakenly assume that poetic devices are only for poetry. In fact, the best prose is full of poetry; it may not rhyme in stanza form, but it is just as beautiful and powerful as any sonnet. Good prose, like good poetry, creates vivid images and is stirring when read aloud. Here are the major poetic devices.

Alliteration. Repetition of initial consonant sounds. *Example: Running rabbit, bursting bubbles, chanting children*

Assonance. Repetition of vowel sounds. *Example: Towel, downy, see, scene*

Hyperbole. Exaggeration. *Example: Her tears filled the ocean. (Caution: Avoid too much hyperbole, or it may be considered "purple prose" or melodramatic.)*

Internal rhyme. Rhyme that occurs within a line, not at the end. *Example: The June moon glowed above.*

Metaphor. Comparison of one thing to another (without using *like* or *as*). *Example: Uncle Malcomb slithered into the room and, at the sight of the visitor, flicked his tongue over his thin, cold lips and darted forward.*

Onomatopoeia. Words that sound like what they are. *Example: Whoosh, buzz, clang, ding-dong*

Personification. Giving human traits to animals or things. *Example: The wind sang an eerie song that night.*

Puns. Words with double meaning. *Example: I named my puppy Van Cliburn because he's the peeing-est (pun on the word pianist).*

Simile. Comparison of one thing to another using *like* or *as. Example: He was as excited as a June bug at a lamppost.*

Synaesthesia. Using one sense to depict another. *Example: Icy silence (touch describing sound); screaming perfume (sound describing smell)*

Understatement. The opposite of hyperbole. *Example: Let's help that little fellow over there (referring to a giant).*

EVOKE EMOTIONS

For most readers, emotions are what make the story enjoyable; otherwise, they might as well be reading a math text or a tax report. Which emotions are evoked depends on the story. They may bring tears, laughter, fear, love or anger. There are several ways the author can bring out emotions.

The five senses. Everyone has felt pain, or hot or cold. We smell sweet roses and rotten eggs. We hear the warble of a thrush or see a golden sunset. We taste homemade vanilla ice cream and ripe, juicey peaches. Using the five senses (touch, smell, hearing, taste and sight) is just one more way to help readers identify with your characters and story. The more sensory descriptions used in a story, the more the reader will identify with the protagonist and feel a part of the story. Becoming part of the story allows the reader to live the story alongside the protagonist. This helps to create emotion: When the hero cries, the reader may also cry.

The following passage from the novel *A Farewell to Arms* by Ernest Hemingway demonstrates how senses evoke emotions:

> . . . In the bed of the river there were pebbles and boulders, dry and white in the sun, and the water was clear and swiftly moving and blue in the channels. Troops went by the house and down the road and the dust they raised powdered the leaves of the trees. . . .

You can *hear* the water, *smell* the dust and *see* the soldiers.

♦ ♦ ♦

You now have the basic tools for writing a great work of YA literature. Now comes the hard part: doing the work, revising it and polishing it until it shines.

Chapter Sixteen

Practice Makes Perfect: The Necessity of Revising

N ovice writers often think they can write perfect copy the first time they apply ink to paper. They whip out a novel and submit the first draft to publishers, only to be rejected. In reality, a novel should be revised many times before submission. Some authors work on one chapter at a time, revising and polishing it to perfection before moving on; others write a complete draft of the novel before starting any revisions. Although I've known authors who write as many as twenty (or fifty or one hundred drafts), for the purposes of this book, let's assume you will be writing three major drafts.

THE FIRST DRAFT (ROUGH DRAFT)

You've probably heard of the left brain–right brain theory: Humans use the right side of the brain for creating artistic matter and the left side for solving problems. An author of fiction must use both sides of the brain. First comes the creative rush— getting the idea and putting it down on paper or mulling it over for several weeks. The rough draft often flows from the pen (or keyboard) fast, furious and creatively. To me, this is the fun part of writing. When I write a rough draft I don't worry about length, spelling, grammar, dates of famous battles or how far away you can hear a cannon boom. My rough draft is so full of gaps and errors, I would not let my dog read it.

Once the rough draft is finished, many authors put it on a shelf for a period of time, oftentimes a few weeks. During this cooling off period, they may work on other projects. If you haven't finished your research, this is a good time to do so. The point is to ignore that manuscript on the shelf, to resist the temptation to work on it. You want to distance yourself from the manuscript so that when you finally do read it again, you will be able to approach it with a fresh and critical eye.

THE SECOND DRAFT (MIDDLE DRAFTS)

The second draft is the most crucial. It is often the most difficult and most time-consuming. The creative half of your brain wrote the rough draft; now the logical side of your brain must identify and repair all the problems. If you compare the writing of a novel to the sculpting of a bust, the first draft is like the lump of clay formed into the rough shape of the head. The second draft is where the majority of the shaping and forming occurs. By the time it is finished, the story is recognizable.

Cut, Cut, Cut

Rarely is the first draft the correct length. Mine is always too long, full of rambling descriptions and pointless dialogue. The second draft is where large, sweeping revisions are made. Entire scenes may have to be cut, superfluous characters deleted, characters and scenes combined, dialogue reduced, scenes moved from one chapter to another, locations or travel methods changed, character personalities recreated or plot segments revised. Cross out unnecessary material and make notes in the margins. It is not uncommon to cut as much as one-third of the rough draft.

Try not to fall in love with your words. Keep in mind that after a manuscript is bought, it goes through at least three or four revisions before it is published. Chances are good that whatever you love the most will be what the editor dislikes. When reading your rough draft, be as logical and critical as possible. Look at the story as if it were written by someone else. If you have a spouse or trusted friend who can give constructive criticism, you may want to ask him to read it and make comments. But in the end, only you can decide what must be done to improve the story.

Lengthen

If your manuscript is too short, look for obvious gaps in the story as you read it. Even a rough draft that is the right length may have serious holes to be filled and can be helped by considering the following: Do the characters need to be fleshed out?

Does the story lack a strong sense of setting and history? Is there too little dialogue? Does it jump from one scene to another too abruptly without a transition?

Research Changes

By the time you begin working on the second draft, you may have discovered from further research that certain scenes are not feasible. For example, *The Silent Storm* is set on Galveston Island, which is reached by crossing a tall bridge spanning Galveston Bay. I have crossed that bridge dozens of times and was sure that the water below was as deep as the ocean. Therefore, in the first draft I had boats doing all kinds of maneuvers in the bay. However, after more research I discovered that the bay is actually only a few feet deep. Because of this information, it was necessary to rewrite all the scenes that involved boats. If you are writing a historical novel, you may learn that a certain weapon, a means of transportation or a household item had not yet been invented.

Oil Your Writing Gears

The second draft is where work on pacing is done, making sure that sequels follow scenes, that there is not too much dialogue in one chapter or too much narrative in another. Work on the dialogue until it sounds natural. Smooth the transitions between scenes and chapters.

Some scenes or chapters require little or no revisions; others will refuse to behave and will drive you nuts. You may find that several middle drafts are needed. If a point is reached where you can't remember what has been changed and you're making things worse rather than better, it's probably time to put the manuscript on the shelf again for a while. There is nothing like approaching the manuscript with a fresh eye for inspiring new revisions.

THE THIRD DRAFT (FINAL DRAFT)

It's time for the final draft when the characters and plot are all satisfactory and all the *major* revisions have been completed. In the final draft you are doing what is commonly referred to as *polishing*. Some authors call this *self-editing*. You are going over the manuscript with a fine-toothed comb, removing all the rough spots. Pay particular attention to the following elements.

Title. Is the title catchy and appealing to an adolescent? Does it reflect the contents of the book (serious or humorous)? Is it unique and enticing?

Opening Hooks. Does the opening scene create a vivid, lasting image? Is it unique and interesting? Does it foreshadow the events of the story?

Cliff-Hangers. Does the chapter end with a "catch"—a question or situation that will compel the reader to continue?

Transitions. Do changes in location and time occur smoothly? Does each scene flow into the next without jarring the reader?

Verbs. Avoid state-of-being verbs: *is, are, was, were* and *be*. Avoid passive verbs. Change imperfect tense and past perfect tense to immediate past tense (i.e., change *was running* or *had run* to *ran*). Avoid vague subjects such as *there was* or *it was*. Avoid weak verbs such as *look, seem, felt* and *appear*. Use strong, descriptive verbs.

Adjectives and adverbs. Avoid excess adjectives and adverbs. Use strong nouns and verbs instead.

Five senses. Use as many of the senses as possible—sight, sound, touch, taste and smell—to make the readers feel like they are there.

Pacing. Vary the length of the sentences—shorter for action and longer for narration. Alternate scenes (where action occurs) with sequels (where narrative occurs). Avoid stringing two or more scenes, or two or more sequels, together. Too many scenes will make the reader feel out of breath; too many sequels will put him to sleep.

Dialogue. Too much dialogue, or boring dialogue, will make the novel seem shallow. Use only enough dialogue to move the story forward. Make it sound natural. Read the dialogue aloud to hear how it sounds. Avoid excessive slang.

Point of view. Most YA novels use one point of view. If you must switch POV, do so in a new chapter, never in the middle of a scene.

Grammar. Check your work against a grammar textbook. Make sure that all the subjects and objects agree. Be certain to use the correct conjunctions for clauses (*that* vs. *which*, *who* vs. *whom*). Check for dangling participles, run-on sentences and misplaced modifiers. Make sure sentences are clear and understandable.

Spelling and Punctuation. Do not depend on a computerized spell-check program. Although it may catch obviously misspelled words, it will not catch words used incorrectly. For example, you may have used *to* when you meant *two* or *too*. Proofread the manuscript carefully.

Tighten. *Tighten* is the term editors use to indicate that excess words need to be cut. Delete all redundant words, phrases or descriptions. If you described the red dress on page 2, there is no need to describe it again on page 3. Most editors have the philosophy of "less is more" and would prefer "He stood" to "He stood up."

♦ ♦ ♦

Congratulations! You are now the proud owner of a YA manuscript. It is a beautiful creation that you will want to share with the world. You have worked long, hard hours researching the subject, writing the rough and middle drafts, and polishing the final draft. A typical YA novel takes about twelve months to write, but some may take years.

After your manuscript is complete, take some time to relax. Reward yourself. You want to be calm and clear-headed for the next step: submitting your manuscript to publishers.

PART FIVE

The Business Side of Writing

Chapter Seventeen

The Voyage Begins: Submitting Your Manuscript

When a manuscript is submitted, it embarks on a long, lonely voyage. It requires tremendous faith and patience from the author while the manuscript is "out there." At times it may seem as if you are at the mercy of heartless editors who enjoy rejecting everything you write. However, you are not as powerless as you think; there are several things you can do to help shorten that voyage.

MANUSCRIPT PREPARATION

An editor once told me that a clean manuscript always got her attention. Why? It lets her know you care about your manuscript, you are professional and understand the rules of submission, and are considerate (a sloppy manuscript is hard on the editor's eyes). A clean manuscript cannot sell a bad story, but a very messy manuscript certainly can prevent a good story from being read.

Several years ago, while judging some unpublished manuscripts, I disqualified the manuscript with the most interesting story because it was in the most deplorable condition—single-spaced with cross-outs, narrow margins, misspelled words and incorrect grammar. Such a manuscript would not survive in the publishing world.

So the first and foremost rule of manuscript submission is: *Be professional.* An author wears many hats, but when it's time to submit your manuscript, leave your emotional hat at the door and become a businessperson. After all, you are selling a product. Here are some basic rules of manuscript preparation.

- **No handwritten manuscripts.** If you cannot type or do not own a computer, hire a typist.
- **Paper.** Use standard white typing paper. No colors, no frills and no erasable bond. The paper need not contain cotton or rag.
- **Margins.** Allow between 1″ and 1½″ on all four sides. The right-hand margin may be either ragged or justified. With today's computers, one format is as easy as the other.
- **Double-space.** Double-space manuscript text. In nonfiction texts, long passages of quotation may be indented and single-spaced.
- **Type fonts.** Use a standard typewriter font such as Courier or Arial. Do not use script or anything fancy or unusual. The story should be able to speak for itself without help from gimmicky fonts.
- **Avoid cross-outs.** With today's computers, it is easy to reprint a page. If using a typewriter, avoid strikeovers and be sure your corrections are not too obvious or messy. A self-correcting typewriter is recommended.
- **Print size.** Standard print size is 12-point. Anything smaller strains the editor's eyes; anything too large may be viewed as unprofessional.
- **Readable print.** Make sure the print is dark and crisp. This means a fresh ribbon if you are using a typewriter, and a fresh toner cartridge if you are using a computer printer. The print should not be blurred, smudged or crooked.
- **Chapter numbers and titles.** Drop down one-third of a page each time you start a new chapter. Type the chapter number and title (if there is one) in all capital letters.
- **Page numbers.** Number the pages consecutively. The upper right-hand corner is the standard location for page numbers.
- **Slug.** In the upper left-hand corner of each page type the title of the novel, or a few words from the title, for identification purposes.
- **Name (optional).** Some authors place their name in the upper right-hand corner in front of the page number, or in the upper left-hand corner following the slug. This is optional.

- **Originals.** With today's computer printers and high-quality photocopiers, it is no longer necessary to send an original. Originals were required in the days when a "copy" meant smudged, pale print made from carbon paper. If you do use a copier, make certain that it is of high quality, with no specks or lines. You can substitute your own typing paper to make it look more like an original.
- **Spelling and grammar.** I reiterate the importance of correct spelling and grammar. This includes hyphenating words correctly. Use the dictionary if in doubt.

RESEARCH THE MARKET

Some authors invest a year or more of their lives painstakingly researching and writing their young adult novels, only to become careless when it comes time to submit the manuscript. Remember, writing is a business. In the end, you are trying to sell a product. If you were trying to sell snowshoes, would you send your samples to Tahiti? No. You would study the market and get addresses of stores and names of contacts in Alaska, Russia and Iceland.

There are several market resources YA authors can study before sending out manuscripts. Your goal is to submit your manuscript to the publishers and editors who will be most likely to purchase your type of work. (See Appendix for addresses of organizations and publications listed in the following sections.)

Market Surveys

A good place to begin your market research is with *Children's Writer's & Illustrator's Market* (published by Writer's Digest Books). It lists children's publishers, with addresses, editors' names, phone numbers, information about the publisher, what areas they are specifically buying, how they pay and, most importantly, their submission policies.

Another thorough source of market information for children's book publishing is the annual *Market Survey* issued by the Society of Children's Book Writers and Illustrators (SCBWI). This publication also offers contact names, pay rates and submission policies, and is free to members of the organization. The Children's Book Council, Inc. will send you a list of children's trade publishers, but it does not contain detailed market information.

Writers Magazines

Another source of market information can be found in publishing- or writing-related magazines. Most have a "market update" section that gives the latest news about which editors are at which houses, which houses are looking for specific materials, which new houses or imprints have just opened and are looking for submissions, which houses have closed and so forth. *The SCBWI Bulletin*, *Publishers Weekly*, *Children's Writer*, *The Writer* and *Writer's Digest* are good places to start.

Publisher's Catalogs

The books a publisher has published are collectively referred to as their *list*. The "frontlist" contains the books being released in the current year; the "backlist" contains books published in previous years. The majority of children's publishers release books twice a year, in the spring and in the fall; therefore, their catalogs are called *Spring* or *Fall* catalogs. They also publish backlist catalogs. For the cost of postage, you may order catalogs directly from the publisher, or you may get them free at major conventions for publishers, booksellers, librarians and teachers.

Go though the catalogs and note the types of books each publisher is releasing. If you cannot find any YA novels, chances are that publisher is not looking for any. If they do have YA books, study them to get a feel for the specific types. Some publishers prefer humor, others prefer multicultural, while still others prefer literary, series books, hardcover only or nonfiction only. You will discover that each publishing house has its own personality, and you will soon realize that your book is more suited to certain houses than others.

Read Recently Published Books

Spend some time in the public library and at a children's bookstore. Better still, visit a nearby middle or high school library. Note what publishers have recently published and which houses are publishing books similar to yours, not just in topic, but also in mood and style.

Read Review Sources

Familiarize yourself with book review periodicals such as *School Library Journal*, *Booklist*, *The Horn Book*, *Kirkus* and *The*

ALAN Review. These periodicals give brief synopses of most of the new books being released. Most school or public libraries subscribe to these periodicals and will let you browse through them.

Check *Children's Books in Print* (*CBIP*)
Study a recent issue to find out what is available that is similar to your book. You may find that a particular publisher specializes in the same topic. The children's department of a public library is a good place to find *CBIP*. Children's bookstores often have copies, too.

LOOK FOR PUBLISHERS RECEPTIVE TO BEGINNERS
Many markets actively solicit new writers. They do not always pay as well as a large publishing house, but the credential of a published book can open doors for you.

Educational Presses
Educational publishers distribute their books to schools and public libraries. You rarely find their materials in retail bookstores. Advances are either nonexistent or very low (five hundred to one thousand dollars). Most presses specialize in hardcover nonfiction. Those that do publish fiction are usually seeking curriculum-oriented pieces—math, writing, social studies, geography and biographies. They are very receptive to beginning writers, especially if you have expertise in the field you are writing about. It is important to study their catalogs, since most of them have many series with specific guidelines. A query is nearly always required. The SCBWI publication *Directory Guide to Educational Markets* is a good source for locating these publishers.

Small Presses (Regional, Religious and Ethnic)
Regional presses specialize in books relating to certain regions of the country. They usually accept both fiction and nonfiction, though YA novels are a hard sell. Advances are typically low, and distribution is limited to the region. *Religious presses* are not always small, but they have specific guidelines. The material they seek is often inspirational in nature. *Ethnic presses* seek books about certain ethnic cultures, and often require that the author be a

member of that culture. Most small presses pay lower advances; some pay royalties on net price. Two SCBWI publications, *Guide to Small Press Markets* and *Guide to the Religious Book Markets*, are good sources of information.

Magazine Markets

Many YA authors get their start by publishing in magazines aimed at teenagers. The subject matter is varied and, in many magazines, includes both fiction and nonfiction. Most have a wide range of word length needs. The pay is usually per word, from a few pennies to fifty cents; you can earn anywhere from fifty to a couple thousand dollars. SCBWI's *Directory Guide to Magazine Markets* is an excellent resource.

Book Packagers

As I mentioned in chapter three, book packagers are always seeking writers for series books. Your ability to write quickly and well is more important to them than your name; in fact, your name may not even appear on the cover, but at three to five thousand dollars per book, you can make a living. SCBWI's *Guide to Book Packagers* is very helpful.

New Imprints and Publishers

An *imprint* (or line) is a branch of a large publisher with its own editorial staff. Sometimes an editor who has earned respect and prestige will be given his own imprint with the authority to select the books he likes. Other imprints cater to particular age groups or topics.

When a new imprint or new publishing company is established, its editors actively seek authors. They read everything that comes in and respond fairly quickly, because they need books to get the line or company started. However, you must act quickly—within months they may be swamped with manuscripts, and within a year will be as bogged down as an older established line or publisher.

The disadvantage of a new line or publisher is that it is untested and may go out of business leaving your book "orphaned." An orphaned book is one whose editor has moved on or whose publisher has folded, leaving no one to promote the book, no one to call about problems and no one who cares about the fate of your baby.

NARROW THE MARKET

After studying the market surveys and the other sources mentioned, you will be able to eliminate over half of the publishers because you will discover that they do not publish YA books. You can eliminate additional publishers depending on the type of book you have written. For example, many do not publish romances, westerns or mysteries. Some do not publish nonfiction; others do not publish fiction. Some pay work-for-hire only, and you may not be interested in that kind of payment. Some do not want "problem" YA books; some are actively looking for multicultural authors. Unfortunately, some publishers will only accept manuscripts submitted by agents. All these aspects help determine who will end up on your short list of publishing houses (make a list of second-choice publishers, too).

After narrowing the field to as few publishers as possible, consider their submission policies. Some will not accept unsolicited manuscripts and some will not accept multiple submissions. Some prefer a query first; others require a proposal. You will have many decisions to make.

WRITE A GREAT QUERY LETTER

A *query letter* is one in which you ask the editor for permission to submit a manuscript or a proposal. Chapter six dealt in depth with query letters for nonfiction projects. A query letter for a work of fiction is similar, with the exception that your occupational experience is not as important. For the longer manuscript of a YA novel, most editors prefer a query. This saves them time and saves you expensive postage. Also, once the editor replies to your query and asks to see the manuscript, it becomes *solicited* and bypasses the *slush pile.*

A query letter is short: only one page with four paragraphs. Unlike the manuscript, a query letter is single-spaced. Here are the contents of a typical query letter.

Salutation. Always address the query letter to a specific editor. (More on how to find the right editor later in this chapter.)

Paragraph One—Introduction. Explain that you are inquiring about the editor's interest in your manuscript. Include the title, word count and age level of the intended reading audience. If it is a collection of short stories, poetry for young adults or one book of a series, mention that; if it is a genre novel (romance, mystery, western, etc.) mention that, also. If you have met the editor in person, heard her speak at a conference, recently read an article written by her or read a market update with her name, cite that information in this paragraph.

Paragraph Two—Synopsis of Story. Briefly explain your story. Using only a few sentences, state name and age of the main character, some background information and the crux of the story. Be as entertaining and compelling as possible, but avoid subjective evaluations such as "This is a wonderful novel about a charming girl . . ." or "I know you'll enjoy this heartwarming novel about. . . ." This is your sales pitch: Be professional.

Paragraph Three—Your Credentials. List any publishing experience you have, including a magazine short story or a poem published in an anthology. Have you taken writing courses under a famous author? Do you have a fine arts degree in writing? Have you won reputable writing contests? Do you work with adolescents in any capacity? Are you a middle-school librarian? Are you the parent of adolescents? Are you an expert in the subject matter (or locale) of your novel? Mention any pertinent professional organizations of which you are a member, for example, Society of Children's Book Writers and Illustrators, Mystery Writers of America or American Association of Beekeepers. If you are widely published, you may enclose a separate sheet called "Author Bio" that lists your expertise and credits.

TIP *Do not say, "My grandchildren love this story."*

Paragraph Four—Closing. Thank the editor for her time and consideration. Let her know that you welcome her suggestions and comments, and that you are willing to make changes.

Return Envelope. Enclose a self-addressed stamped envelope (SASE) for a reply.

Return Postcard (Optional). As I mentioned in chapter six, some authors enclose a self-addressed stamped postcard rather than a SASE. This is more convenient for the editor because it does not require her to compose a letter of response. The card has several advantages: (1) You now have the name of a specific editor to send the material to; (2) the editor may write pertinent information on the card that will be useful in the future; and (3) response time is usually faster than when enclosing a SASE. (For a sample return postcard, see Appendix.)

WRITE A GREAT COVER LETTER

A *cover letter* accompanies a proposal or manuscript sent to the editor. There are two types of cover letters. One accompanies an *unsolicited* submission and looks almost exactly like a query letter. But rather than asking the editor "would you be interested in" or "may I send you my manuscript," say "please find enclosed for your consideration my manuscript entitled. . . ."

The second type of cover letter accompanies a *solicited* submission. In this case, an editor has read your query and has asked you to send the proposal or manuscript to her. This cover letter is very brief with no more than two paragraphs. Thank the editor for requesting the enclosed manuscript. Let her know you are open to suggestions and willing to make changes. You should also mention if the manuscript is a multiple submission. However, you need not explain where else it has been submitted. A simple sentence such as, "Another publisher has also requested to read this manuscript" is sufficient.

TIP *When submitting solicited work, write "Requested Manuscript" on the outside of the envelope.*

SASE. Always enclose a return envelope with adequate postage.

Acknowledgment card. Some authors also enclose a SAS postcard to let them know that the editor received the manuscript. If you leave a few lines for comments, editors will often give you an estimate of how long it will take them to get back to you.

TIP *Just because your postcard has not been returned does not mean that the manuscript did not arrive. Some editors have a heavy backlog of mail, and it may take a while for your manuscript to even be opened.*

Record keeping. Keep an index card file (or a bookkeeper's ledger) with the following information: name of manuscript, publisher and editor, and date of submission and comments, if rejected. This becomes crucial if you have several manuscripts and have submitted them to many publishers.

CONSIDER SENDING A PROPOSAL

The *proposal* (or partial) for a YA novel consists of the cover letter, a synopsis or outline and the first three chapters.

Synopsis vs. outline. A *synopsis* is an engaging summary of the story, written in present tense and double-spaced. It tells the story chronologically. In other words, perhaps the reader will not find out until chapter three of the novel that the hero is the illegitimate son of a wealthy senator, but in your synopsis you may mention that fact right away. Use a compelling, interesting writing style that suits the mood of the novel. A synopsis may even contain a few brief quotes to demonstrate the dialogue. For a YA novel of 50,000 words, a seven to ten page synopsis is typical. Remember that the purpose of the synopsis is to high-light the main points of the story, not to provide detailed descriptions of minor points.

On the other hand, some editors may request a proposal containing a *chapter-by-chapter outline*. In an outline, the events of each chapter are briefly summarized using present tense and devoting about one-half to one page per chapter (depending on the chapter's length). If your chapters are short, you may summarize more than one chapter on an outline page. If you are writing a historical novel, you may also include a page or two of background information about the time period.

There are advantages to submitting by proposal rather than sending an entire manuscript. The proposal requires less postage to submit, the editor can read it faster and you can submit without investing months or years of effort into completing a novel. All of my novels, except one, were sold based on proposals. Of course, selling on proposal does not mean immediate payment; you will not receive the full advance until you complete the manuscript, which may be a year later. On the other hand, the editor may want the completed manuscript immediately, so be prepared. You may be asked to finish the novel sooner than you ever dreamed.

ARE MULTIPLE SUBMISSIONS ACCEPTABLE?

A *multiple submission* is a manuscript which has been submitted to several publishing houses at the same time. Some publishers have a policy of not accepting such submissions; others do not mind. Some authors consider multiple submissions unethical, while others consider them practical. Only you can decide what is right for you. The important thing is to be honest with the editor. If it is a multiple submission, inform her. Let the editor decide whether to take the chance on your manuscript or send it back. As long as you are honest and forthright, no one can accuse you of unethical behavior.

One type of multiple submission you want to avoid, however, is the infamous "shotgun" method. This means sending out the manuscript to every publisher listed in *Writer's Market*. That may mean as many as thirty or forty publishing houses. This is not only a sign of a rank beginner, it is a waste of time and postage. The section of this chapter called "Research the Market" (see page 159) explains how to target your manuscript to the right publishers.

NOW COMES THE WAITING GAME

Every author should have the middle names *Patience* and *Hope*. In the best of all worlds, your manuscript will arrive at the publisher, be read immediately and create joy in the heart of the editor—and you will receive that exciting phone call within one week. Unfortunately, this rarely happens; out of the twenty-five books I have sold, such a prompt response has happened to me only twice.

In the real world, your manuscript arrives at the publisher, is logged in, and then begins the long, slow process of working its way to an editor's hands. In the past, a first reader (usually a recent English major graduate) read through the slush pile (unsolicited manuscripts). She divided them into the good, the bad and the maybe. Most were returned with rejection form letters; the rest were sent on to editors. In those days, some editors had assistants who read the manuscripts and culled them even further.

Today, publishing companies have downsized, cutting personnel. The typical editor is overworked and may have no assistant.

She may have to read all of the manuscripts addressed to her, and some from the slush pile addressed to "Dear Editor." She will cull them herself, and compose and write her own rejection letters. At a small press, the editor may also be the owner, secretary, salesman and bookkeeper.

Reading new submissions is only one tiny part of an editor's job. When she receives manuscripts in the mail, she puts them aside to read in her "spare" time. Often, this spare time does not come until evenings or weekends when she is at home. She reads constantly, and a manuscript with small, faded or blurry print will not be well received, nor will one full of typos, crossouts or strikeovers. That is why a clean, neat, readable manuscript is so important.

What this all means is that the typical YA manuscript will take at least three months to be read, and often longer. If the editor likes the manuscript, she will take it to an editorial meeting and get input from other editors and the sales force. If a decision is made to purchase the manuscript, mathematical formulas are used to determine how many copies should be printed, the retail price of the book and the amount of the advance to offer the author.

All of this is time-consuming, which explains why many editors do not like multiple submissions. If they go to this much trouble and call to make you an offer only to find that you have sold the manuscript elsewhere, they have wasted many hours of work.

TIP *As soon as you sell a manuscript, notify every publisher to whom you have submitted the manuscript.*

If you have not heard from the editor in three months, follow up with a polite letter inquiring about the status of your manuscript. If you do not receive a reply within another month, you can either withdraw the manuscript or leave it there and keep waiting. If you have given an editor the exclusive right to read the manuscript and then decide to submit it elsewhere after three or four months, be certain to notify the editor that you are doing so.

Two of my books sold after waiting periods of one year each. My longest wait was eighteen months. Yes, eighteen months felt like forever, but when the manuscript finally came back to me, it was accompanied by a long, detailed letter full of useful suggestions and a request to see the revised manuscript.

> **TIP** *Don't burn bridges. Always be professional and courteous, venting your anger on the cat, not the editor. Editors move from house to house and have excellent memories.*

REJECTION IS PART OF A WRITER'S LIFE

You will inevitably receive a rejection. Every author does. It cannot be avoided any more than a baby can avoid falling when she is learning to walk. Even after twenty-five books, I still get rejections and, yes, they still sting. But I have come to realize that they are part of a writer's life, just like bad weather and dogs are part of a mailman's life.

Do not dwell on the rejection. Allow yourself no more than one day to mope. Vent your anger by jogging, punching a pillow or mowing the grass (pretend the blades of grass are the editors' heads). Don't call or write to the editor in anger; you will regret it later. Talk to writer friends who have had rejections, and be supportive when they call you. More importantly, do not let rejections depress you to the point of giving up. Take that manuscript and make changes if you want, but send it out again as soon as possible. As long as it is out there, there should be hope in your heart. If it is laying on your desk, it will *never* be published.

Not all rejections are created equally. If you receive a personal rejection letter, this means the editor considered your work and presentation a notch above the others rejected that week. It takes time to compose and write that letter. Consider it a compliment. The same goes for a handwritten note scribbled on a rejection card or letter. If you receive a rejection letter with suggestions for changes and an indication that the editor would be interested in reviewing the work again, write a letter immediately stating you will make the changes and send the revised manuscript as soon as possible. If the editor's letter makes only vague suggestions with no indication of wanting to see it again, you may write a thank-you letter and ask if she would like to see the revised manuscript when it's ready.

Remember: *All criticism is subjective.* Many times I have received a rejection telling me that the book just didn't work or wasn't "right for our list," only to find an editor elsewhere who loved and bought it. Some of the most famous and beloved novels were rejected time and time again before being published.

If you are persistent and patient, if you continue to practice and improve, and if you carefully research the market, the day will arrive when the phone rings and the editor says she wants to make you an offer. Suddenly, all the pain and frustration fade away and you will be the happiest person in the world. In fact, you are about to become a new persona: a published author.

Chapter Eighteen

Let's Make a Deal: Contracts, Editors and Agents

W hen the editor calls, your first instinct is to whoop and holler and say yes to every single offer she makes. Don't do that. Take a deep breath and be calm. Though your heart is pounding, let your head rule. Show enthusiasm, but tell the editor you would like to think about it for a day or two and get back to her. The editor will not get upset and withdraw the offer; she will not think you are greedy. Instead, she will respect you for your professionalism.

You should have studied contracts so that you can ask some intelligent questions. Even if you have decided to take the advance offered, you should ask questions nonetheless. Most publishers have what is called a *boilerplate contract*, a standard form sent to all authors. Although most aspects of the contract will be nonnegotiable, some may be flexible. You should secure the best deal you can. The following information will help.

THE ADVANCE

An *advance* is money paid to the author against royalties projected to be earned by the book. In other words, it is a loan given to the author by the publisher, traditionally for the purpose of allowing the author to exist while the book is being prepared for publication (a process that can take a year or more). The author will pay the advance back to the publisher out of the royalties earned when the book begins to sell. The first royalty statement is usually a negative amount because the book has not yet earned enough money to cover the advance.

To illustrate, let's say the publisher advanced you $5,000 with a royalty rate of 10 percent of retail. A year and a half later when you see the first royalty statement, you see that one thousand copies sold for $15 each, earning a total of $15,000. Your royalty cut is 10 percent, or $1,500. But since this is not enough to pay back your original $5,000 advance, your statement will reflect that you still owe the publisher $3,500. It may take two or three royalty statements for the book to earn enough to repay the advance. During that time you receive no money.

Unfortunately, many YA novels do not even earn the advance and, therefore, are eventually taken out of print. In such cases, the author does not have to repay the publisher. However, this does not look good on your record and the publisher might be hesitant to buy your next book. On the other hand, if the book wins a major award or is well reviewed, it may earn out the advance on the first royalty statement. The money earned on all future statements is then yours to keep. A successful hardcover book may go back to press once or several times, each one called a *printing*.

Advances are usually broken into multiple payments; for example, half on delivery of the completed manuscript and the other half on final acceptance of the manuscript. Final acceptance means that you have made revisions (usually several sets) to the editor's satisfaction, and the book is ready to go into production. Occasionally, the advance is split into three payments with the final payment being paid upon publication of the book.

When you call the editor back, don't be afraid to ask for a higher advance if you feel that the one offered is too low. (See chapter nineteen for statistics on advances.) This is a business deal. No matter how much the publishing house loves your book, they want to acquire it for the lowest price possible. They know that most first-time authors are excited and naive and will accept any offer made. If you set the precedent of being an author who accepts a low advance, don't be surprised if advances stay low on future books. On the other hand, if you show that you are a knowledgeable and intelligent businessperson, you are more likely to receive advances that increase as you publish more books.

By telephone, the editor will make you an offer stipulating the advance and royalty rate. Six to twelve weeks later (time varies with each publisher) the contract will arrive. If you accept the advance and royalty rate verbally, it is considered unethical to increase the price after the contract arrives. If, for some reason, you have decided that the advance is ridiculously low, you always have the option of refusing to sign the contract. The advance, however, is only one aspect of the contract. There are many other facets that you need to understand before negotiating.

ROYALTIES

A *royalty* is the percentage of the book's price that the author is paid each time a copy of the book sells. There are two types of book prices. Royalties based on *retail price* (or list price) are calculated by the price listed on the book's cover and in the publisher's catalog. This is the price you usually find in bookstores. A typical hardcover YA novel has a list price of $13.95 to $15.95; a typical YA paperback costs from $3.95 to $5.95. Even if the bookstore discounts the book, you will receive your royalty based on the list price.

On the other hand, *net price* is one from which the publisher has deducted its expenses (postage and handling, for example), the price at which the book was sold to the vendor or the discounted sale price. Each publisher's contract has its own definition of net price. The difference between retail and net may be a dollar or more per book and can represent a large loss of income. Avoid net royalties when possible; be aware, however, that most educational and smaller presses pay on net, and rarely will they make exceptions.

Royalties are usually paid every six months. The two most common accounting periods are January through June and July through December. However, don't expect to see your royalty statement a few days after June or December 30. In fact, many major publishers allow themselves four months to accumulate the figures and prepare the statements. Therefore, for the January through June period, your statement will arrive some time between October 1 and October 31. Smaller presses are usually faster because they have lower overhead and fewer authors.

With major publishers, the standard royalty rate for a hardcover YA book is 8 to 10 percent of the retail price; paperback royalties are usually 6 percent. Although royalty rates are often not negotiable in the boilerplate contract, the publisher is usually willing to escalate the rate as book sales increase. For example, the first 25,000 copies would be 10 percent; the next 25,000 would escalate to 12 percent. However, selling over 25,000 copies is a very strong showing for the YA category and rarely happens.

SUBSIDIARY RIGHTS

From time to time the publisher will sell an interested party the right to publish your book, or parts of it. This is called a *subsidiary right* (or subright). The most common subsidiary rights are book clubs, foreign languages, movie and TV (dramatic rights), paperback rights, serial rights (magazines and newspapers), audiotapes, anthologies, textbooks, computer uses, special editions for promotional premiums and license of characters for merchandise (e.g., dolls, toys and coloring books).

Money received for subsidiary rights will be divided between the publisher and the author, sometimes 50/50 and sometimes 25/75. Try to negotiate for the largest amount you can get. This may earn you a few hundred extra dollars. For example, if a French publisher buys the right to publish a French version of your novel for three hundred dollars, you would receive one hundred fifty dollars if the rights are split 50/50. Some publishers allow you to retain certain rights, such as serial rights or dramatic rights, especially if you have an agent with contacts in Hollywood.

One of the most important subsidiary rights is paperback rights. As some publishers do not have a paperback line, their contract will include a clause stating that if another publisher buys paperback rights, the terms will be negotiated at that time. Other publishers have their own paperback lines and, if you aren't careful, they can print your book in paperback form without paying you a nickel. With these publishers, make certain that your contract agrees to pay you an advance for paperback rights up front. This is called a *hard/soft deal*—the publisher is simultaneously buying both hardcover and paperback rights from you. A higher advance (one to two thousand dollars more) should be paid for this right. If your contract does not address paperback rights, add a clause stating that the advance and royalty terms will be negotiated at a later time.

AUTHOR'S COPIES

Most contracts specify a certain number of free copies to be given to the author (typically ten). This is one term that is easily negotiated. Ask for as many copies as possible; you can usually get twenty-five without too much of an argument. When these copies are gone, you will have to purchase your own books (usually at a 40 percent discount), so free copies can be quite a savings. Also, don't forget to ask for copies of the paperback editions when they are released. As for foreign editions, don't expect more than two or three copies. If your contract does not mention free copies, insert an addendum.

OPTION CLAUSE

The option clause is of benefit to the publisher. It requires you to submit your next book to them exclusively. They then have the right to consider your book and turn it down at their leisure. Always delete the option clause. If you like your editor and publisher, it is only natural that you will send them your next literary work. If the publisher refuses to budge on the option clause, at least add words that limit it, such as "next historical YA novel." This frees you to send your nonhistorical YA books to other publishers. Also, add a clause limiting the amount of time the publisher has to consider the work. Most importantly, make sure that the terms for the next book will be negotiated separately from the current one.

MULTIBOOK CONTRACTS

The multibook contract looks great on the surface, but it can be a trap for the inexperienced author. For example, let's say your multibook contract agrees to buy your next three YA novels. The good points are (1) you are fairly well assured that you will have three books published (although publishers do have the right not to publish the future books if they find the books unsatisfactory); (2) you will receive partial advances for three books up front; and (3) you will have steady work for the next several years.

The bad points are (1) the advance for the future books is now set at what is most likely a low-end rate; (2) your editor may leave or you may discover that you do not like the publishing house; and (3) you may lose interest in the books you promised to write, in which case you face years of drudgery. Should your first book do extremely well (perhaps it wins a major award), you would not be able to negotiate better terms for your next two books, as you would have been able to do had you signed a single-book contract. If you do sign a multi-book contract, ask that each successive book receives an advance greater than the last.

REVERSION OF RIGHTS

Another clause that can sometimes be negotiated is the *reversion of rights* clause which stipulates that if your book goes out of print, you can ask for your rights back and sell the book elsewhere. The publisher sometimes gives itself a long period to respond—up to six months. If they let a book go out of print, you have every right to get it back.

COPYRIGHT

You do not have to worry about taking out a copyright on your work; the publisher will do that for you. However, do be certain that the contract states the copyright will be in your name. Fight for this. Otherwise, your book does not belong to you and the publisher can do as it pleases with your work in the future. Some work-for-hire publishers and small presses use this method and are not flexible. If the publisher refuses to process the copyright in your name, realize that you are giving up many of your rights as an author.

PUT IT IN WRITING

Although I have addressed the major aspects of contracts, they contain many more details. Always read your contract thoroughly, even if it is twenty pages long. Some authors hire attorneys who specialize in literary contracts. I lightly pencil notes in the margins, or use Post-its, when I question something. Do not hesitate to ask your editor to explain the wording or unfamiliar terms. Some editors are contract knowledgeable; others may refer you to the contracts department.

As with any business deal, get all your terms in writing. Even if the editor has agreed to something verbally on the phone, it must be stated within the contract to be valid. You can write agreed-to changes on the contract in ink and initial them. If many changes are made, the contracts department may rewrite the contract with the changes and return it to you. This delays the receipt of your advance, but in the long run you are better off.

From the time you verbally accept the advance and royalty rate, it may take several weeks for the contract to arrive. The average is about two months, but some larger publishing houses take six to eight months. Once you have signed the contract, you will wait several more weeks (or months) before you receive the first part of your advance. Therefore, it is conceivable that with some larger houses you will wait one year before receiving the money. By then, the book is usually completed and well on its way to production.

THE ROLE OF THE EDITOR

The most important person in your career during the making of your book will be your editor. The editor reads your manuscript and makes revision suggestions; guides you to meet the editorial standards of the publishing company and answers your questions; and releases your advance money when you have met the obligations of the contract.

The typical editor is working on several projects at once, each in a different stage of development. After reviewing contract negotiations in the morning with you, she may work on first revisions with another author and finalize galleys with yet another, in addition to discussing the dust jacket with the illustrator and writing flap copy. She must attend editorial and sales meetings; compose letters; make calls to agents, authors and other editors; prepare speeches or slide presentations for conferences; and meet with agents. She must also read your manuscript several times and write lengthy letters with suggestions on how to improve the manuscript. And somewhere in there she must find time to read new submissions.

In other words, editors are busy. They deserve the respect given to any hardworking professional. They do not deserve your anger and confrontations. It is possible to disagree with an editor about a suggestion without becoming defensive and hostile.

I have written both adult and children's books, and have found that children's editors are the most thoughtful and considerate group in the industry. Many authors develop close friendships with their editors, even following them to a new house when the editor leaves. This brings up the downside of editors: They move around a lot. Gone are the days when editors stayed with publishing houses for twenty or thirty years. This is a reflection of the times we live in. Because of this, you can expect your editor to quit or change houses a few times during your career.

AGENTS

A discussion of writing is not complete without mention of literary agents. Some writers feel that they cannot possibly succeed in a writing career without an agent, but there are two sides to every coin.

Side One. A good agent will do all of the unpleasant work associated with negotiating the contract and haggling with the editor for more money. He can be assertive and not jeopardize your relationship with the editor; you, on the other hand, may be timid about asking for more money for fear of making the editor angry. A good agent has contacts with many publishing houses; he knows the editors and what types of manuscripts each one prefers. A manuscript submitted by an agent *always* gets read, often faster than one sent over the transom (some publishers accept only manuscripts submitted by agents). To attract higher offers, an agent may put a terrific manuscript up for auction—something an author rarely does on his own. Also, a good agent networks at every opportunity and gets your name out there every time he meets someone new; will go over your royalty statement to make certain that it is correct according to the terms of the contract; and will be honest and tell you if he thinks a manuscript requires more work before being submitted.

Side Two. An agent will take 15 percent of your income (a few will take only 10 percent, but that is rare). He must divide his time between several clients and may have only a few minutes per day for you. He may sit on your manuscript for months, or lose interest if it does not sell right away. An agent will take away most of your control regarding where the manuscript is to be sent. He may be unable to get an advance higher than you would have on your own, but you still owe him the 15 percent. (Advances for first-time authors are often inflexible, even when an agent is involved.) If you have "bad vibes" and sever your relationship, the agent still receives 15 percent of the royalties for the life of the book. Usually, the agent receives the money first and then writes you a check for your portion of the royalties, thereby creating room for financial errors. If the agent is not liked or respected within the publishing industry, editors may not buy the books he submits. A bad agent is worse than no agent at all.

Some of today's most famous children's authors do not use an agent. In the long run, only you know if you need one. Finding a good agent is very difficult. The best are usually not accepting unpublished clients; the unknowns are usually struggling to survive. I have sold twenty books on my own and five with the help of an agent. I found both methods to have their advantages and disadvantages.

If you decide you want an agent, search for one who specializes in children's books and has knowledge of the YA market. Many agents belong to the Association of Authors' Representatives. And while New York agents are closer to the industry, they are not necessarily better. The best advice is to get references. Ask around. And listen to agents who speak at conferences. Your gut instinct is usually correct. The SCBWI publication *SCBWI Guide to Agents* is an excellent source of information and a comprehensive list of agents who will represent children's and YA authors. (See Appendix for a list of reference books about literary agents and for addresses of organizations that can provide lists of literary agents.)

EDITORIAL SUGGESTIONS FOR REVISIONS

As mentioned earlier, your editor will read your manuscript thoroughly, writing a lengthy letter with suggestions for revisions. She will also write in the margins and apply Post-it notes covered with comments. For novels, the first set of revisions typically requires you to retype the manuscript. The second set often involves solving problems of plot and characterization. The third set, usually smaller in scope, requires tightening rather than substantial changes.

After the editor is satisfied with the manuscript, she sends it to a copy editor. The copy editor checks the manuscript for grammar and spelling, for accuracy, and for consistency and logic. For example, you may have a scene in which a hawk flies at someone during the night, when in fact hawks are daylight birds. Or, you may describe the heroine's mother-in-law as a redhead on page 3, but call her a brunette on page 75. Copy editors pose dozens of questions, but often revisions require only a word inserted or deleted here and there. You usually do not know who the copy editor is and do not communicate directly with him. You return the final revised manuscript to your editor. Smaller publishers may use the same editor throughout the entire process.

In the meantime, you will receive color proofs of the cover artwork. If you are lucky, you will have seen the rough sketch and been allowed to make suggestions. A blurb will have been written for the inside flap of the dust jacket (or the back of a paperback). Ask to read it, and also the author's bio.

After the copyediting, the next time you see the manuscript it will be in galley form. *Galleys* are the typeset manuscript set in the same size print that the book will appear. You are in the homestretch now. You will proofread the galleys, looking for typesetting errors and any mistakes you may have made. This is the last time you will have an opportunity to make changes. Most contracts stipulate that if the author makes more than 10 percent changes, the author must pay for the excess typesetting. (For hardcover YA novels, the galleys you proofread have already been bound with a temporary paper cover. These are called *uncorrected proofs* and are sent to book reviewers at major review journals months before the book is released.) Once the corrected galleys leave your hands, you will not see the book again until it is the finished product.

There is nothing more thrilling than holding your author's copy, seeing your name on the cover, smelling the ink and reading the words that now miraculously look so awesome. It is a moment to savor—and to remember when, somewhere down the road, you begin to wonder, as all writers do, is it worth it?

Chapter Nineteen

The Writing Life: Is It Worth It?

N ot long ago I was rushed to the emergency room with severe stomach pains. Ten days later, I was rushed back, this time for a false heart attack brought on by anxiety. All my problems were caused by stress. When the doctor asked me what my occupation was and I told her "author of children's books," she was shocked. "I thought that kind of work was stress free," she said. A common misconception.

As any self-employed person will tell you, the stress of not having a steady paycheck, medical insurance or fixed working hours can fray the nerves and churn the stomach—especially those first few years when the income is seldom enough to support a dog, much less you and a family.

Some people write for therapeutic reasons and do not care if they are published. Other people have set the goal of being published and do not care if the book makes money. If you fall into one of those categories, you will not be as concerned with the financial aspects of being a writer. However, if your goal is to become a full-time author, to support yourself and perhaps your family, too, then you need to take a long, realistic look at the income potential of YA authors.

CAN I MAKE A LIVING AT THIS?

Karen Cushman's first novel, *Catherine, Called Birdy*, was a Newbery Honor Book; her second novel, *The Midwife's Apprentice*, won the 1996 Newbery Award. She was fifty years old before she started writing and was truly an overnight success. But her story is the exception to the rule.

More commonly, the YA author climbs the mountain inch by inch by selling several books and getting solid reviews, gradually receiving higher advances and name recognition. Gary Paulsen, one of the most famous YA authors today, wrote many adult novels and lived close to the poverty level for many years before one of his YA novels won a Newbery Honor Medal and brought his talent into the limelight. The majority of YA authors (or most authors, for that matter) are not able to support themselves by writing. Most have another source for income: a day job, retirement pension or wealthy spouse.

So how much money can you expect to make from a YA book? A first hardcover YA novel commands an advance between $3,500 and $5,000 from a major publishing house. An original paperback usually generates an advance of between $2,500 and $4,000. Small presses and educational presses offer much lower advances, ranging from nothing at all to $2,000. There are exceptions, of course. A strong first book placed on the auction block by an agent might bring $10,000 to $20,000. But on average, if an editor offers you $5,000 for your first YA novel, consider yourself lucky.

Remember that the publisher is taking a big chance with an unknown author. The cost of printing a book may run $30,000 or more, depending on the number of copies printed. If the publisher does not recoup these costs, it loses money. If this happens too many times, the company will go out of business.

After an author becomes established, the amount of the advance will rise in direct proportion to the success of previous books. An author with consistently high *sellthrough rates* (the percentage of books sold compared to the number printed) is considered a good risk. If your books are breaking even or making marginal profits, your advance will not increase by leaps and bounds. On the other hand, it's safe to say that if you win the Newbery Award, your next novel will receive a nice big advance. Name recognition is a key factor in the amount of the advance.

As for royalties, 10 percent is considered normal for a YA hardcover novel or nonfiction book published by a major publishing house. Some publishers will insist on 8 percent until you have proven yourself. Less than 8 percent from a major publisher should be questioned. The standard royalty rate for a paperback original is 6 percent, but again, some publishers will try to go as low as 4 percent for that first book. Small presses and educational presses often pay as low as 5 percent—and this is nearly always based on net price. As mentioned previously, try to include an escalation clause for your royalties.

DON'T QUIT YOUR DAY JOB

I was shocked when I spoke with an author who had over thirty books to her credit, many of them award-winning. She told me that $20,000 in earnings was an extremely good year for her. One of the worst mistakes you can make is to quit a paying job too soon. Most Americans cannot exist on $5,000 a year—the average advance for one YA novel. Even if your book does extremely well, that first royalty statement and check will not arrive until several months after the book is released. And even if you sell two books in one year, that is only $10,000, still not enough for most of us to live on.

This sad state of affairs is why so many new authors drop out in the first two or three years. They become enraptured with inflated visions of success after publication of a single book. They quit their regular jobs, convinced that their careers as successful authors are now ensured. But selling one book does not guarantee selling a second.

If you quit your job too soon, your funds may run out, your bills will pile up and you will become frustrated. You may become grumpy, feel guilty, develop writer's block and hear the clock ticking every time you sit at the keyboard, a sound that may cause you to produce drivel and turn you into a bundle of nerves. Finally, you may return to a "real" job, swearing you will never again try to be an author. At this point, another writing career may end.

I was in that boat after publishing two adult books. I begrudgingly returned to work, determined that I would try again someday. When I did try again, I knew not to quit my day job until I was financially able. I waited until I had published four books, had two more under contract and had one year's minimum income in my savings account. After four more years, and nine published books, I finally reached an income equivalent to that of an entry-level secretarial job. It was not until one of my picture books received national awards, appeared on the *Reading Rainbow* television program and was placed on a major reading list that I began to make a decent income.

Once you have quit your day job, you will find that in addition to writing and selling your books, you will probably need to supplement your royalty income. One of the most common ways is through speaking engagements.

SPEAK AT SCHOOLS

Children's authors are luckier than authors in adult fields because of the potential for income from speaking at schools. Most major school districts across the United States (and in many foreign nations) bring in authors once or twice a year. Because my first three novels were for adults, I was not aware of this lucrative market during the release of my first children's book. When a local school librarian invited me to speak at her school, I said no thanks. My fear of speaking in front of a class (or auditorium) full of children was right up there with the fear of death. Soon other schools called. I continued to turn them down until another children's author told me that she made more money from school visits than from all of her advances and royalties combined. Indeed, famous authors often charge one or two thousand dollars a day. At that rate, you can earn in one week what it took one year to earn from book sales.

I got my feet wet by agreeing to speak for free at a summer school. I figured that if they didn't like me, at least they had not wasted their money. I spent hours preparing for my one-hour program and thought I would die of anxiety before the day arrived. As it turned out, I not only survived, but actually enjoyed it. So did the kids, counselors and teachers. I gained confidence, and the next time a school called I said yes and charged fifty dollars for the day. As more area schools hired me, I increased my price. The year my picture book did so well, I spoke at about one hundred schools and several national conferences. My income more than quadrupled that year. As my books won more national awards, I began to speak out of state. I now speak across the United States and at schools abroad.

Publishers love an author who speaks at schools, because most schools will sell the visiting authors' book(s) to their students. (The author should expect to autograph their books.) I have sold as many as five hundred books at one school. Naturally, your sellthrough rate will go up, as will the amount of the royalty check. Your visit is also a form of promotion. All of the students who hear your presentation will now know your name and be more likely to buy and read your books. They may ask for your books at local bookstores, increasing your sales there, too.

The downside to speaking at schools is that you may finally reach the point where it will interfere with your writing too much. Also, speaking at schools demands a high level of energy and stamina. When I visit a lot of schools, I typically contract several illnesses. In one school year's time I had strep throat twice, bronchitis three times, tonsillitis twice and several colds. Many successful authors balance school visits with time spent on writing, speaking at conferences and research.

What fee should I charge? Unless your first book wins a major award or appears on a state award list, you should expect to start at the bottom of the fee scale. Your fee also depends on where you live. Generally speaking, schools in the northern and eastern parts of the United States pay higher honorarium fees than in the south, midwest and west (except for California). Where I live, a fee of $200 per day is average for a beginning author. Authors of some stature receive between $300 and $500. The two very famous authors who live in my hometown request as much as $1,500 to $2,000 per day. You may need to experiment a few times to find the right price. Ask other area authors what they charge. And naturally, it should increase a little as your fame increases.

Who arranges school visits? The majority of school visits are arranged by the school's librarian or media specialist. The presentation is often held in the library or media center. Occasionally, the PTA will organize author visits, especially when it is paying the expenses. Rarely does the principal make the arrangements. Your best bet is to contact the librarian. Even if she is not in charge, she will usually know who is. Some of the larger school districts have consortiums of several schools that coordinate and share expenses to bring in an author for a week or more. In this case, one coordinator may handle all the arrangements for many schools.

How do I arrange school visits? Most authors start with local schools, especially if they have children in the school system. Call the librarian, or visit in person and show (or give) her a copy of your book and a brochure. Tell her your fee and let her know that you are eager to speak in area schools. Since a librarian prefers an author who writes for the grade levels that attend her school, you will mostly visit intermediate, middle and junior high schools (grades five through nine). High schools, on the other hand, rarely sponsor author visits.

Mail your brochures to schools within driving distance or to towns you know you will be traveling to in the near future. You can obtain addresses of schools and the names of librarians from most state library associations. There are also professional organizations that will sell you lists of schools (see Appendix); however, mass mailings can be quite expensive and are not proven to be effective.

Another way to advertise yourself to schools is to add your name to a list of speakers. If you belong to SCBWI, check with your local chapter; many chapters maintain Speaker's Bureau lists and mail them out to area schools. There are books for librarians that list authors' names and addresses; for example, *Something About the Author* and *The Address Book of Children's Authors and Illustrators*. Most children's publishers produce a brochure for librarians that lists authors who speak at schools. Ask your publisher to be placed on its list.

Network and keep your business cards handy. Some school districts hold monthly librarian meetings. Ask the school district president if you may take a few minutes at the beginning of one of their meetings to introduce yourself and your book. Librarians are always looking for new blood. Attend local conferences of librarians and teachers, and hand out brochures and cards.

Offer to do a few charity presentations to get your name in the system. If you do a great job, the librarian will talk about you at the library meeting. A referral is the best way to secure a school visit.

What do I talk about and how long should I talk? Most librarians want you to talk about writing and to inspire the students to read. Often your visit will be part of a reading incentive program. For example, students who read a certain number of books will be able to attend your presentation. Most author presentations include basics such as how the author got started, where ideas came from and how the author researched and wrote the book. You may also be asked to talk about the subject matter of your book, especially if it is nonfiction.

Some authors bring along props, such as slides or items related to the subject matter of the book. Several of my books deal with the Vietnamese culture, so I bring artifacts from Vietnam, along with slides. Encouraging the students to participate always livens things up. The average presentation for older students (grades five and up) is forty-five minutes. Be sure to allow time for questions and a brief break between each presentation. (I use the break time to scrub my hands with antibacterial soap—one way to help prevent the spread of germs.) Junior high students are often too embarrassed to ask questions in front of their classmates, so you may want to have them write down their questions ahead of time.

What about other speaking engagements? You may also be asked to speak at conferences for writers, teachers and librarians. Honorariums for such functions depend on how large the conference is and how bad you want to participate. When you are invited, ask if your expenses will be paid. Well-known authors charge between one and two thousand dollars or more for a speech or workshop at a conference, and have all expenses paid. If the conference cannot afford to pay your expenses, at least have them waive the conference fee, provide your meals and allow you to sell your book. Conferences are not only enjoyable and more like a vacation than work, they are also a great way to network.

If you fear public speaking, you are not alone. The book *I Can See You Naked* says that public speaking is the number one fear of most people. But you will overcome your fear after realizing that the audiences want to hear what you have to say. You may want to take a course in public speaking, often available through local colleges or continuing education programs. You can practice on your family, spouse, writers group or friends. Start with small groups, perhaps speaking for free. Your first few speeches or workshops may be at local conferences, your payment nothing more than a free lunch or dinner, but any speaking engagement will be good exposure.

PROMOTE YOURSELF

Many authors do no promotion after their first book is released. They have the attitude that the advance is the only money they will ever receive for the book and the book will either sink or swim on its own. They place the first book behind them and immediately dive headlong into writing the next one. This may be especially true of series books, where the number of sales is more or less set and nothing you can do will increase or decrease that amount.

In many ways, this "it's out of my hands now" attitude is the healthiest and least stressful one an author can take. However, now that you are an author, your income depends on how many copies of your books sell and how many speaking engagements you contract. Here are some ways you can increase public awareness of you and your books.

Make Brochures and Business Cards

The first thing you should do is to make an attractive brochure. With today's computers, it does not need to be expensive—black-and-white print on textured or colored paper is sufficient. I like a trifold brochure made from $8\frac{1}{2}'' \times 11''$ paper. Include a brief author bio, information about your book(s), your photo, the book jacket(s) or some artwork, and a brief description of what kind of talks you give and the grade levels you speak to. Include your address, telephone and fax numbers, and E-mail address. Also make business cards. Keep the brochures and cards handy (for example, in your car or briefcase) to give to any teachers, librarians or booksellers you meet.

Attend Conferences

Every state has a library association and most have an annual conference. This is a great place to hand out your brochures and business cards and to network with librarians. Ask the conference chairman to set up an autographing session for you, and make sure that your books are available to purchase. Your publisher may or may not make the arrangements, depending on the size of the conference. You can also rent a booth and display your books and brochures, but this may not be cost-effective as the booth may cost several hundred dollars.

The American Library Association conventions (one during the summer and another in January) are very large and draw librarians from across the United States. Ask your publisher to arrange an autographing session for you (hopefully, the publisher will pay for your travel and hotel expenses, too). While you are autographing, hand out your brochures and business cards.

Writers conferences are often looking for published authors to speak. The pay is usually low—often only expenses and one hundred dollars—but the exposure will increase your name recognition and book sales.

Other conferences and conventions that welcome YA authors include: National Council of Teachers of English (NCTE), International Reading Association (IRA), Texas Library Association (TLA—the largest state library conference in the United States) and BookExpo America (BEA—formerly American Booksellers Association). Many of these organizations have state or regional chapters with smaller regional conferences.

Book Signings

Visit area bookstores and show them your book. Ask the buyer to carry it, and let them know you will be happy to autograph. However, do not expect huge crowds to show up. Even the best-advertised autograph session rarely stimulates big sales. Several large chain booksellers have told me that selling five books is considered a successful event. Autograph sessions at schools and conferences are much more rewarding. But again, don't expect large lines for your first book unless it has won major awards.

The Internet

As more and more people make use of the Internet, an author's opportunity to advertise grows by leaps and bounds. Many authors have their own Web sites. It can be as colorful, entertaining and informative as your imagination. Some authors hire professionals to construct the Web page, including biographical information about the author, a list of books and sometimes short synopses, photos of dust jackets, information about school visits, your E-mail address and a post office box for regular mail (do not include your home address and phone number). Think of it as a multipage brochure. Instead of handing it out at conferences, it is available to hundreds of thousands of Internet users. Because the potential exposure is so great, it's an opportunity that anyone with a computer and modem should not pass up.

Newspapers, Radio and TV

Send a copy of your book to your area newspaper(s) (or ask your publisher to send one), to the attention of the book reviewer. Or call the reviewer and introduce yourself. Contact reporters who write feature articles. They are often looking for interesting local people. If your book has a local slant, mention that.

If your local radio and TV station(s) have a talk show, send a promotion packet and copy of your book. Even a two-minute interview will get your name to several hundred potential buyers.

Networking

Whenever you attend functions, talk to people and mingle. You never know what great contacts you may make, and don't be afraid to talk to other authors, editors or agents at conference lectures and parties. Remember, however: Do not be obnoxious or pushy. Being polite and courteous are more impressive.

Book Reviews

Your publisher will send out review copies to all the major sources. You should also make a list of regional sources and ask the publisher to send copies to them, too. This list may include area newspapers, magazines or any publication that reviews local authors.

Bookfairs and Charity Events

Many schools hold annual bookfairs to raise funds for the school library. Books are spread out on tables, often in the library or gymnasium, for several days. The event will often climax with a supper and authors autographing their books. I never charge area schools for appearing at their bookfair for an hour or two; free food and the smiling faces of children are my reward. It is a great way to promote yourself, sell your books and, nine times out of ten, the librarian will ask you to speak to the students (for money) sometime in the future.

Closely related are charity events. You may be asked to autograph or even donate a signed copy of your book for an auction. I always try to comply, knowing that my book and name will be in the limelight for a short while.

Awards

One of the quickest ways to bring your book to the attention of teachers and librarians is to win prestigious awards. Of course, every author would like to win the Newbery, but the competition is fierce. Also, the award is usually given to a book for middle-grade readers rather than older young adults. The American Library Association (ALA) selects several books each year for its Best Books for Young Adults (BBYA) list, and also selects ALA Notable Books in various age categories. The Children's Book Council selects books for various lists; for example, Notable Children's Books in the Field of Social Studies. The New York Public Library compiles a list of Best Books for the Teen Age, which many nationwide teachers and librarians consult. The Society of Children's Book Writers and Illustrators sponsors the annual Golden Kite Award, which has both novel and nonfiction categories. And, the Scott O'Dell Award is presented to the best historical children's book. Major publishers automatically enter your books in these contests, but check with your publisher to make certain that they do.

Many national writers organizations have annual contests for published members that include a YA or children's category. For example, Western Writers of America has the Spur Award, Romance Writers of America has the Rita Award, Mystery Writers of America has the Edgar Award and science fiction books receive the Nebula Award. If your book falls into one of these categories, you can ask your publisher to enter your book, or you may enter it yourself.

One of the best ways to increase sales and name recognition is to be placed on a state reading list or a state "reader's choice" list. These lists are compiled by state library associations and usually contain books for different age categories. In many states, students read the listed books and vote for their favorite. The winner later receives an award which is often presented at a banquet at the state librarian's association annual conference. For example, Texas has the Bluebonnet List and the Lone Star Reading List; California has the Young Reader's Choice Award; and Ohio has the Buckeye Award. Even if your book does not win, just appearing on a list increases sales, since librarians try to have at least one copy of each book for students to read. To be considered for a list, your book must be nominated. Nominations are usually submitted by librarians, but some states allow any interested party (even the author) to suggest books to be considered. (See Appendix for a list of books that contain addresses of contests and awards.)

THE TAXING SIDE OF AN AUTHOR'S LIFE

An author is a small businessperson. Even before you sell your first book, you need to keep exacting records of all your expenses. Keep them all in one place so they will be easy to tabulate at the end of the year. Typical tax-deductible expenses include office supplies and equipment, postage, home office (percentage of your house used for the office and phone bills, utilities or rent), books and reference materials, mileage traveled for research, research photographs, mileage traveled to and from libraries, subscriptions to writers magazines, professional organization dues, conference fees, writing courses, school visit props, hotels and a percentage of meals during research trips.

You must fill out several IRS forms, including Schedules C and SE. You must also fill out an automobile depreciation or standard mileage form and an Office Use of Home form. If you make a profit, you will not only pay income taxes, but also Social Security taxes (15.3 percent rather than the 7.65 percent that an employed person pays). You may end up paying as much as 17 percent of your gross income toward taxes. If you do not have a head for business and taxes, you may prefer to hire a tax accountant. Try to find one who has thorough knowledge of a writer's unique situations.

Most importantly, clearly label every receipt. When I visit schools and speak about the country of Vietnam, I show the students banana leaves and Vietnamese bananas, coconut pods, sugar cane and bamboo shoots. This may look like a grocery list to most tax accountants unless it is labeled as a school visit expense. Also, keep a mileage log in your car indicating where and how far you have traveled. Documentation is your first line of defense if you are ever audited.

If you sell your own books, even to friends and relatives, you must obtain a sales tax ID number from your state. The state requires that you collect sales tax on any books you sell and then send the money to them. Even if you don't charge tax to your friends, you still must pay the state tax out of your own pocket. For example, if the retail price of your book is $15.00, a state sales tax of 10 percent would be $1.50, making the final price of the book $16.50. If you tell a friend, "Oh, I'll sell it to you for just $15.00 and no tax," you will still owe $1.50 to the state. In most states, penalties for not collecting sales taxes can be very steep.

IRS forms and tax laws can be very confusing. Don't rely on an over-the-phone answer from an IRS employee. They rarely know what to do with an author who does not fit neatly into any one category. IRS publications relating to self-employment are available free of charge and are essential when filling out your 1040. The book *The Writer's Tax Guide: Writing and Writing It Off*, by Michael Arthur Jones (Veritas Publishing Co., 1997), contains a lot of useful information.

ANTICIPATE BAD DAYS

It is not uncommon to fall into a slump when reality sets in and you realize that you will not become rich and famous overnight, when bad reviews (or no reviews) come or when good reviews don't seem to increase your sales. All of this is to be expected. Many YA novels barely earn out the advance, much less become best-sellers. This does not mean that your book is a failure or poorly written; this is just a characteristic of the YA market. There are fewer young adult readers than middle- and elementary-age children, and they do not want to pay fourteen dollars for a hardcover book. Authors of paperback YA novels face a fierce, competitive market where shelf space is limited and name recognition is equivalent to big sales.

Rejections. After your first book has been published, you may think you will never receive another rejection letter. Not so. My editor has rejected some very famous authors whose work was not compatible with the publishing house, or because a similar book was just purchased. After twenty-five books, I still receive rejections. The pain of rejection never goes away completely, but the recovery period shortens as you become more experienced.

Try to focus on the positive. The editor is not rejecting you, the writer, but that specific story at that specific time. Many years ago, I submitted a manuscript to an editor who, though she liked it and responded with a nice letter, turned the work down. Two years later, I sent the manuscript out again, not including her publisher because of the rejection. I was shocked to receive a phone call from her making an offer. She had changed companies and the manuscript fit her new publisher's needs.

Bad reviews. Nothing can cheer up an author faster than a good review in a national review source. You are on top of the world; others have read your work and found it brilliant—or at least entertaining. On the other hand, a bad review can hurt your book sales and destroy your confidence. You have been compared to others and found lacking. The reviewers have missed the point of the story, included incorrect information, and even have the names of your characters wrong.

What should you do? Fire off an angry letter to the reviewer? Call and complain to your editor? The best course of action is to do nothing. Believe it or not, experts say that even a bad review is better than no review. People will often remember the title of the book or your name but forget what the reviewer said. Keep in mind that reviewers (mostly librarians and literature teachers) are expressing personal opinions. Two may hate your book, but chances are that two others will love it. Most librarians will read several reviews before drawing a conclusion and selecting books, and realize that reviews are often slanted toward a personal bias. Finally, a bad review will not necessarily affect sales if your book is one of a series or if you are already an established author with a following.

Writer's block. In a way, writer's block is just another form of depression. Many writers become blocked after convincing themselves that they are untalented and anything they have to say is meaningless. Writer's block often takes the form of diversions—cleaning the house, bathing the dog or changing the oil filter—anything utilitarian to keep them from writing. During these times, rather than dwelling on perceived failures, start plotting your next book. For example, go to the library and check out a stack of books on a particular research topic; it will give you a sense of direction. Just thinking about a new project can take away the blues.

But don't stay away from your writing too long. Procrastination is probably the writer's worst enemy. The longer you are

away, the harder it is to start again. If your novel is in the dol-
drums, give yourself permission to write something other than
the novel in progress. Try poetry for a while or a short story—
or even a picture book. Record your daily thoughts. Often the
process of fingers striking the keyboard is enough to lift you
out of the dumps.

Remind yourself that everyone must start at the beginning.
Some of the most famous authors have received horrible reviews
or worked for peanuts the first few years of their literary careers.
It is all part of the game. Every job has its ups and downs; writing
is no different. You must tell yourself that for every down, there
will come an up. Then eat a box of chocolates.

SO, IS IT WORTH IT?

I have mentioned some of the downs of being an author; now
it's time to hear about some of the ups. There is the joy of a
great review, of being invited to speak at schools or conferences,
of autographing books, and of receiving large advances and
healthy royalty checks.

Perhaps the greatest joy of writing for children and young adults
is hearing from your audience. They are loyal, passionate and often
awestruck. They will never write to say they hate your book. Even
if it is a class assignment, they try to find something good to say.
Always respond to fan letters. Sure, the children don't put in a
SASE, and sometimes they ask you to send a free copy of your
book, but you have a responsibility to your readers. Just a quick
thank-you note, or even a colorful postcard, will keep you in good
stead with them. And believe me, a devoted fan will read your
books and tell everyone else to read them, too.

Once you have received a few fan letters, your writing life will
take on a new perspective. You will realize that the words you
write have the power to mold young minds. Here's one of my
favorites, from a seventh-grade Vietnamese-American girl, Kris-
tine, who read *Song of the Buffalo Boy* and *Shadow of the Dragon*.

> *Shadow of the Dragon* and *Song of the Buffalo Boy* made
> me realize how proud and lucky I am to be Vietnamese. It
> also makes me realize how fortunate I am to live in a house,
> to have clothes on my back, shoes on my feet and food to
> eat.

It makes me feel good to read a book that doesn't make Vietnam a bad place to be. I hope I can go to Vietnam sometime in the future.

Another favorite came from an eighth-grade boy named Matt, who read *Shadow of the Dragon.*

This book made me think differently about Vietnamese people. I always thought they were mean. (I guess I was a racist.) I didn't know what hardships they had to go through. I didn't know that they risked their life to come over here. They want to be free just like us. Now I hope that I can be friends with more Vietnamese.

And finally, a seventh-grade boy named Lucas, who also read *Shadow of the Dragon,* touched me with this letter:

I don't know if your book was meant to tell the reader this but it reminded me of all the racists. Racists are doing bad things to good people just because of race . . . When the task of reading your 300-page book first started, I didn't want to read it (I'm not the reading type). After I started it, I could hardly put it down. I read it in about 4 days. That's a record for me. . . .

That, my friend, is what writing for young adults is all about. It is not just the size of your advance or the rate of your royalties. It is knowing that what you do is meaningful and worthwhile and that young adults may remember you and your stories long into adulthood. They may even follow the examples set by your characters. And when those bright-eyed students giggle and squirm while asking you to autograph their copy of your book, in your heart you will know that, in spite of all the struggles and agony of being an author, it is worth it.

ORGANIZATIONS OF INTEREST TO WRITERS OF YOUNG ADULT BOOKS

Society of Children's Book Writers and Illustrators
345 North Maple Drive
Suite 296
Beverly Hills, CA 90210
www.scbwi.org
The above address is for the national headquarters. Most states have one or more regional chapters. Here are some of the publications SCBWI provides to its members:
Answers to Some Questions About Contracts
Copyright Facts for Writers
Guide to Agents
Guide to Book Packagers/Producers
Guide to College/University/Community Courses in Writing and Illustrating
Guide to Educational Markets
Guide to Foreign Markets
Guide to Magazine Markets
Guide to Religious Book Markets
Publishers of Books for Young People/Market Survey

The Children's Book Council, Inc.
568 Broadway, Suite 404
New York, NY 10012
www.cbcbooks.org
This nonprofit organization makes several publications available, including a list of children's book publishers. Much information is contained in their Web site. Write for their catalog of publications.

American Library Association
50 East Huron Street
Chicago, IL 60611
www.ala.org

International Reading Association
800 Barksdale Road
P.O. Box 8139
Newark, DE 19714-8139

National Council of Teachers of English (NCTE)
1111 West Kenyon Road
Urbana, IL 61801-1096
www.ncte.org
This organization holds an annual conference in late November. State chapters also hold conferences. Their subgroup, ALAN (Assembly on Literature for Adolescents), specializes in young adult literature and publishes the ALAN Review.

MAGAZINES OF INTEREST FOR WRITERS

Children's Book Insider
254 East Mombasha Road
Monroe, NY 10950

Children's Writer
95 Long Ridge Road
West Redding, CT 06896-1124

Once Upon a Time . . .
Audrey B. Baird, Editor
553 Winston Court
St. Paul, MN 55118

Publishers Weekly
245 West 17th Street
New York, NY 10011

The Writer
120 Boylston Street
Boston, MA 02116-4615

Writer's Digest
1507 Dana Avenue
Cincinnati, OH 45207

GENERAL REFERENCE BOOKS FOR CHILDREN'S WRITERS

Bicknell, T.P. and F. Trotman. *How to Write and Illustrate Children's Books.*

Buening, Alice, ed. *Children's Writer's & Illustrator's Market.*

Gates, Frieda. *How to Write, Illustrate, and Design Children's Books.*

Giblin, James Cross. *Writing Books for Young People.*

Irwin, Hadley, and Jeannette Eyerly. *Writing Young Adult Novels.*

Karl, Jean E. *How to Write and Sell Children's Pictures Books.*

Litowinsky, Olga. *Writing and Publishing Books for Children in the 1990s: The Inside Story from the Editor's Desk.*

Roberts, Ellen E.M. *The Children's Picture Book: How to Write It, How to Sell It*; also *Nonfiction for Children: How to Write It, How to Sell It.*

Seuling, Barbara. *How to Write a Children's Book & Get It Published.*

Stanley, George E. *Writing Short Stories for Young People.*

Tierney, Susan, ed. *Children's Writer Guide.*

Tomajczyk, S.F. *The Children's Writer's Marketplace.*

Woods, Bruce, ed. *The Basics of Writing for Children & Young Adults.*

Woolley, Catherine. *Writing for Children.*

Wyndham, Lee, and Arnold Madison. *Writing for Children & Teenagers.*

Yolen, Jane. *Guide to Writing for Children.*

Zinsser, William, ed. *The Art & Craft of Writing for Children.*

SPECIALIZED REFERENCE BOOKS

Agents and Contracts
Balkin, Richard. *A Writer's Guide to Contract Negotiations.*
Curtis, Richard. *How to be Your Own Literary Agent: The Business of Getting a Book Published.*
Flowers, Mary. *A Writer's Guide to a Children's Book Contract.*
Larsen, Michael. *Literary Agents: What They Do, How They Do It, and How to Find and Work With the Right One for You.*

Proposals and Query Letters
Buchman, Dian, and Seli Groves. *The Writer's Digest Guide to Manuscript Formats.*
Cool, Lisa Collier. *How to Write Irresistible Query Letters.*
Larsen, Michael. *How to Write a Book Proposal.*

Words, Grammar and Self-Editing
Brohaugh, William. *Write Tight: How to Keep Your Prose Sharp, Focused and Concise.*
Gross, Gerald, ed. *Editors on Editing: What Writers Need to Know About What Editors Do.*
Lewin, Esther and Albert. *The Random House Thesaurus of Slang.*
Lunsford, Andrea, and Robert Connors. *St. Martin's Handbook.*
McCrum et al. *The Story of English, New and Revised Edition.*
Research & Education Association. *Barron's Essentials of English Language.*
Rude, Carolyn. *Technical Editing.*
Shefter, Harry. *Short Cuts to Effective English.*
Stein, Sol. *Stein on Writing.*
Strunk, William, and E.B. White. *The Elements of Style.*
University of Chicago Press. *The Chicago Manual of Style.*
Venolia, Jan. *Write Right!*

Useful Research Resources
American Booksellers Association. *The ABA Children's Bookselling Resource Handbook.*
Dickson, Paul. *Timelines: Day by Day and Trend by Trend from the Dawn of the Atomic Age to the Gulf War.*
Lane, Megan, ed. *Photographer's Market.*

Lesko, Matthew. *Information U.S.A.*

McCutcheon, Marc. *The Writer's Guide to Everyday Life in the 1800s.*

Panati, Charles. *Panati's Extraordinary Origins of Everyday Things.*

Purcell, Ann and Carl. *Stock Photography: The Complete Guide.*

R.R. Bowker. *Literary Market Place.*

Author Promotion and Marketing

Armstrong, Charles. *Information Marketing: How to Profit: Selling Information in the 1990s.*

Boe, Anne, and Bettie Youngs. *Is Your "Net" Working?: A Complete Guide to Building Contacts and Career Visibility.*

Floyd, Elaine. *Marketing With Newsletters,* 2nd ed.

Gallardo, Evelyn. *How to Promote Your Children's Book: A Survival Guide.*

Kremer, John. *Book Publishing: A Bibliography and Resource Guide.*

Raab, Susan S. *An Author's Guide to Children's Book Promotion.*

School Visits and Speeches

Blount, R. Howard, Jr. *The Address Book of Children's Authors and Illustrators: Corresponding With the Creators of Children's Literature.*

Frank, Milo O. *How to Get Your Point Across in 30 Seconds or Less.*

Hoff, Ron. *I Can See You Naked: A Fearless Guide to Making Great Presentations.*

Melton, David. *How to Capture Live Authors and Bring Them to Your Schools.*

Contests and Awards Resources

Buening, Alice, ed. *Children's Writer's & Illustrator's Market* (annual publication that lists contests in back).

PEN American Center. *Grants and Awards Available to American Writers.*

Tierney, Susan, ed. *Children's Writer Guide* (annual publication that lists contests).

MAGAZINES FOR YOUNG ADULTS

Alive Now!
Blue Jean Magazine
Boy's Life
Breakaway
Brio
Campus Life
Career World
Careers and Colleges
Challenge
Choices
Cicada
Cracked
Exploring
For Graduates Only
For Seniors Only
Guideposts for Teens
Keynoter
Listen Magazine
New Era
On Course: A Magazine for Teens

Scholastic Math
Scholastic Scope
Science World
Seek
Seventeen
Spirit
Sports Illustrated for Kids
'Teen
Teen Life
Teen People
Teen Power
Teenage Christian
Tiger Beat
Visions
YM
Young and Alive
Young Salvationist
Young Scholar
Youth Update

WEB SITES OF INTEREST FOR CHILDREN'S WRITERS

The Internet is constantly changing, with new material being added and old deleted. The Web sites below have links to other Web sites of use to children's authors and writers in general. I suggest connecting with the Purple Crayon or Children's Literature Web Guide first.

- Bookwire Index—Children's Publishers:
  www.bookwire.com/index/Childrens-Publishers.html
- Center for Adolescent Studies:
  www.education.indiana.edu/cas/index.html
- The Children's Book Council:
  www.cbcbooks.org
- Children's Literature Web Guide:
  www.ucalgary.ca/~dkbrown/
- The English Teachers' Web Site:
  www.mlckew.edu.au/english
- Inkspot:
  www.inkspot.com/bookstore/child.html
- Purple Crayon:
  www.underdown.org
- Raab Associates:
  www.raabassociates.com

REVIEW SOURCES FOR CHILDREN'S & YOUNG ADULT BOOKS

The ALAN Review
Book Links
Booklist
Bulletin of the Center for Children's Books (often called *The Bulletin*)
The Horn Book
Journal of Adolescent and Adult Literacy
Kirkus Reviews
NCTE English Journal (TALL: Teaching and Learning Literature)
Publishers Weekly
School Library Journal
Voice of Youth Advocates (VOYA)
Voices From the Middle
Young Adult Library Services Association (YALSA)

SAMPLE CORRESPONDENCE

Sample Query Letter

November 6, 19XX

Ms. (Editor's name)
Avon Books for Young Readers
105 Madison Avenue
New York, NY 10016

Dear Ms. (Editor's name):

I enjoyed hearing you speak at the Golden Triangle Writer's Conference in Beaumont, Texas, last month. You mentioned that you are interested in mysteries for middle-grade and young adult readers. I have just completed a novel, THE YELLOW ROSE MYSTERY, which has approximately 35,000 words and is aimed at children ages eight through twelve.

The novel's protagonist, thirteen-year-old Lennie Cooper, expects to see dead roses, not dead people, when she temporarily takes over her brother's flower delivery job in thier small hometown. And the last person she expects to confess to the murder of a shady character like Johnny Jako is honest, shy Jody Chandler, a fifteen-year-old rodeo contestant in town for the annual Pioneer Days Festival and Rodeo. Lennie is sure Jody is innocent and sets out to find the real murderer, with her only clue—a bouquet of yellow roses.

My writing background includes two adult novels (Berkeley Publishing) and eight books for children. One of my young adult novels won the 1990 Guilded Quill Award in Juvenile Fiction, as well as a works-in-progress grant sponsored by Judy Blume and the Society of Children's Book Writers and Illustrators. See attached bio sheet for more details.

If you would like to read the manuscript or an outline and sample chapters, please return the enclosed postcard at your earliest convenience. I look forward to hearing from you in the near future.

Sincerely,

Sherry Garland

enc: SAS Postcard

Sample Cover Letter

November 21, 19XX

Ms. (Editor's name)
Avon Books for Young Readers
105 Madison Avenue
New York, NY 10016

Dear Ms. (Editor's name):

Please find enclosed my young adult novel, THE YELLOW ROSE
MYSTERY, which you recently requested to see.

Thank you in advance for your time and consideration. I always welcome suggestions and am willing to make any changes necessary to meet Avon's editorial standards. At this time, another publishing house is also considering this manuscript.

I look forward to hearing from you at your earliest convenience.

Sincerely,

Sherry Garland

enc: Yellow Rose Mystery,
    Acknowledgment card

Sample Self-Addressed Stamped Reply Postcard (Accompanies a query letter)

The Yellow Rose Mystery

_____ Yes, please send me the complete manuscript.

_____ Yes, please send me the proposal only.

_____ No, we are not interested at this time.

_____   _____
Signature   Date

Comments _____

_____

_____

Sample Acknowledgment Card (Accompanies a manuscript)

The Yellow Rose Mystery

I have received the above manuscript (proposal).

_____   _____
Signature   Date

Comments _____

_____

_____

_____

_____

TIPS FOR BREAKING INTO THE CHILDREN'S PUBLISHING MARKET

FOUR BASIC STEPS TO BEING PUBLISHED

1. Write the best manuscript you can.
2. Develop credentials so editors will be more likely to read your work.
3. Research the market so you will send your manuscript to the appropriate publisher.
4. Submit your manuscript in its best form.

Step One: Write It

Develop your writing skills. Do not send a manuscript until it is your best work.

1. Take a writing course (through local universities; private lessons or workshops).
2. Join a critique group or writers club.
3. Subscribe to writers magazines.
4. Read writing technique books for basics and manuscript preparation.
5. Read children's books like the ones you want to write.
6. Write as much as possible, and rewrite each piece several times.

Step Two: Develop Credentials

This lets editors know that you are serious about writing for children. It doesn't guarantee that they will buy your book, but helps to ensure that your book will get read more quickly and thoroughly.

1. Join professional writers organizations (SCBWI is the best).
2. Attend writers conferences and workshops—meet editors.
3. Enter writing contests.
4. Write for children's magazines (fiction and nonfiction).

Step Three: Research the Market

This helps to ensure that the publisher you submit to is buying your type of manuscript. Each publisher has preferences—

no young adult, lots of humor, multicultural, environmental, etc.

The following list offers advice on researching the children's publishing market.

1. Study market guides such as those provided by the SCBWI.
2. Study market updates in magazines (*Writer; SCBWI Bulletin; Children's Book Insider; Children's Writer*).
3. Study publishers' catalogs.
4. Look at current books in libraries or bookstores to determine which houses are publishing books like yours.
5. Narrow the market.
6. Some publishers are more receptive to novice writers:
   a) Educational presses (limited payment and distribution)
   b) Regional presses (limited payment and distribution)
   c) New publishers or new imprints of established publishers
   d) Book packagers (Daniel Weiss; MegaBooks; Cloverdale)
   e) Specialty publishers (religious, ethnic)

Step Four: Submit a Well-Prepared Manuscript

Be professional and neat. Think of your query letter as a resume and your manuscript as a job interview.

1. Query letter should be brief and to the point—one page long.
2. Enclose a self-addressed stamped postcard for the editor's reply.
3. If your manuscript is requested, enclose a brief cover letter (double-spaced typing, no errors and neat appearance) and a SASE.
4. Keep records of your manuscript's submission history.
5. Always be courteous and professional.
6. Multiple submissions are OK if the publisher permits. Inform the editor if the manuscript is a multiple submission.
7. For picture books, do not enclose illustrations or suggestions (unless you are a professional illustrator) and do not send a dummy—the publishing house will choose the illustrator. Send double-spaced straight text.

INDEX

More Great Books
to Help You Get Published!

You Can Write Children's Books—In this book for first-time children's writers, you'll learn to follow the important writing and submission guidelines necessary to get your work in print. It includes information on today's hot trends, targeting the right age group, types of nonfiction and attention getting tips for manuscript submission. *#10547/$12.99/128 pages/paperback*

Ten Steps to Publishing Children's Books—This excellent reference turns the mysterious process of getting published into an easy, step-by-step method. Vital information is provided to assist you in polishing the skills necessary to make your dreams come true. *#10534/$24.95/128 pages*

Children's Writer's Word Book—A quick-reference book providing you with everything you need to ensure that your writing speaks to a young audience. It includes a thesaurus and guidelines for sentence length, word usage and themes appropriate for each reading level. *#10316/$19.99/352 pages*

Writing and Illustrating Children's Books for Publication—Delightfully illustrated, each lesson includes imaginative writing and illustrating exercises, along with reading lists, self-editing checklists and case studies. *#10448/$24.95/128 pages*

1999 Children's Writer's & Illustrator's Market—This invaluable reference provides annually updated information on where to sell your writing and illustrations for children. Included are 260 book publishers, 125 magazines, 140 contests and awards, plus 200 conferences and workshops. *#10582/$19.99/368 pages/paperback*

The Writer's Digest Sourcebook for Building Believable Characters—Professional tips and a huge thesaurus of human traits to help you create unforgettable characters make this reference a "must have" for any writer. *#10463/$17.99/288 pages*

Creating Characters—The detailed instruction in this book illuminates the basics and fine points of successful fictional characters: traits, relationships, motivations, emotions, humor and strong dialogue. *#10417/$14.99/192 pages/paperback*

Writing Dialogue—This excellent text is distinguished by the engaging voice, good humor and authoritative instruction of Tom Chiarella. Whether it's an argument, a love scene or a kids' powwow, Chiarella provides you with demonstrations that show how to write exchanges that sound realistic. *#48032/$14.99/176 pages/paperback*

English Through the Ages—You'll love this comprehensive reference that features the birth dates of more than 50,000 words, from Old English to modern-day slang. With this book on your writing table, you'll never again worry about linguistic anachronisms, while at the same time adding flair and accuracy to your writing. *#10540/$24.99/608 pages*

The Writer's Guuide to Everyday Life in the Middle Ages—This writer's companion will guide you through the medieval world of Northwestern Europe. Discover the facts on dining habits, clothing, armor, festivals, religious orders and much more—everything you need to paint an authentic picture. *#10423/$17.99/256 pages*

The Writer's Guide to Everyday Life in Renaissance England—If your writing takes you into Renaissance England, you'll find your details here. Discover the fashions of the day, what people ate, table customs, family life, city life, piracy, what the Royal Court was like and more. *#10484/$18.99/272 pages*

The Writer's Guide to Everday Life in the 1800s—From clothes to food, social customs to furnishings, you'll find everything you need to write an accurate story about this century. Plus, the entries are dated so you won't invent something before its time. *#10353/$18.99/320 pages*

The Writer's Guide to Everyday Life in Regency and Victorian England—You'll save hours of valuable research time and achieve historical accuracy as you reference slice-of-life facts, anecdotes and first-hand accounts of 19th century England. Included are such illuminating details as food, recipes, customs of courtship, popular slang and common occupations. *#10545/$18.99/240 pages*

Grammatically Correct: The Writer's Guide to Punctuation, Spelling, Style, Usage and Grammar—This superior reference arms you against spelling errors and related problems. It also emphasizes why, in the age of spell-checkers, you must still know how to spell. Easy, quick and comprehensive, this handy volume will also show you how to write prose that's clear, concise and graceful. *#10529/$19.99/352 pages*

Roget's Superthesaurus, Second Edition—With more than 400,000 words, including 2,000 + new and expanded entries, this book offers you more features than any other word reference on the market. It also features a time-saving "reverse dictionary" and sample sentences. *#10541/$19.99/672 pages/paperback*

Discovering the Writer Within—A 40-day "workout program" of imagination-stretching exercises that will help throw open your inner doors, release your creativity, discover surprising connections and spark fresh ideas. These exercises will nudge your originality into stimulating, new explorations. #10472/$14.99/192 pages/paperback

How to Write and Sell Historical Fiction—Finally, a guide that addresses the unique challenges you face in researching, writing and marketing your historical fiction. Covered are the fundamentals for creating accurate and compelling literature about the past. #10502/$17.99/224 pages